THE NEW YORK PUBLIC LIBRARY

ITS ARCHITECTURE AND DECORATION

THE CLASSICAL AMERICA SERIES IN ART AND ARCHITECTURE
Henry Hope Reed and H. Stafford Bryant, Jr., General Editors

W. W. NORTON & COMPANY, INC.

The American Vignola by William R. Ware

The Architecture of Humanism by Geoffrey Scott

The Classic Point off View by Kenyon Cox

The Decoration of Houses by Edith Wharton and Ogden Codman, Jr.

The Golden City by Henry Hope Reed

Fragments from Greek and Roman Architecture
The Classical America Edition of Hector d'Espouy's Plates

Monumental Classic Architecture in Great Britain and Ireland by Albert F. Richardson

The Library of Congress; Its Architecture and Decoration by Herbert Small

What Is Painting? and Other Essays by Kenyon Cox (in preparation)

Man As Hero: The Human Figure in Western Art by Pierce Rice (in preparation)

WITH THE ARCHITECTURAL BOOK PUBLISHING COMPANY

Student's Edition of the *Monograph of the Work of McKim, Mead & White, 1879–1915*

Letarouilly on Renaissance Rome The Student's Edition of *Paul Letarouilly's Edifices de Rome Moderne* and *Le Vatican et la Basilique de Saint-Pierre* by John Barrington Bayley

Architectural Rendering in Wash by H. Van Buren Magonigle (in preparation)

On Videotape

Drawing of the Classical: A Videotape Series Devoted to the Drafting of the Five Orders by Alvin Holm (in preparation)

Classical America is the society which encourages the classical tradition in the arts of the United States. Inquiries about the society should be sent to Classical America, in care of W. W. Norton & Company, Inc., 500 Fifth Avenue, New York, N.Y. 10110

THE NEW YORK PUBLIC LIBRARY

ITS ARCHITECTURE

AND DECORATION

HENRY HOPE REED

PHOTOGRAPHS BY ANNE DAY *(unless otherwise noted)*

PREFACE BY ARTHUR ROSS

CLASSICAL AMERICA · THE ARTHUR ROSS FOUNDATION

W · W · NORTON & COMPANY

NEW YORK   *LONDON*

The text of this book is composed in Bembo, with display type
set in Bauer Bodoni. Composition by Vail-Ballou Press, Inc.
Manufacturing by Murray Printing Company. Book design
by Margaret Wagner.

FIRST EDITION

Reed, Henry Hope.
    The New York Public Library: its architecture and
decoration.

    (Classical America series in art and architecture)
    1. New York Public Library.   2. Library architecture
—New York (N. Y.)   3. Decoration and ornament, Archi-
tectural—New York (N. Y.)   I. Title.   II. Series.
Z733.N43 1986   027.4747'1   86-5394
ISBN 0-393-02317-6
ISBN 0-393-30336-5 (pbk.)

W. W. Norton & Company, Inc., 500 Fifth Avenue, New York, N. Y. 10110
W. W. Norton & Company Ltd., 37 Great Russell Street, London WC1B 3NU

1 2 3 4 5 6 7 8 9 0

For Constance

CONTENTS

FOREWORD *by Arthur Ross* *xi*

ACKNOWLEDGMENTS *xiii*

I   INTRODUCTION *3*

II   THE APPROACH AND THE TERRACE *35*

III   THE FACADE *47*

IV   THE PORTICO *59*

V   ASTOR HALL *65*

VI   THE GOTTESMAN EXHIBITION HALL *73*

VII   THE SOUTH–NORTH GALLERY. DEWITT WALLACE PERIODICAL ROOM.
MAP DIVISION. SCIENCE AND TECHNOLOGY RESEARCH CENTER *89*

VIII   THE NORTH STAIRWAY. SLAVONIC DIVISION. ORIENTAL DIVISION.
ECONOMIC AND PUBLIC AFFAIRS DIVISIONS. SECOND FLOOR
GALLERY *109*

IX   THIRD FLOOR LANDING. STOKES GALLERY. BERG EXHIBITION ROOM.
      BERG COLLECTION. ARENTS COLLECTION. PRINT GALLERY. ART REFERENCE
      ROOM. PRINTS, PHOTOGRAPHS AND SPENCER COLLECTION. RARE BOOK ROOM.
      EDNA B. SALOMON ROOM   *125*

X   CATALOG ROOM.   *137*

XI   MAIN READING ROOM   *145*

XII   UNITED STATES HISTORY, LOCAL HISTORY, AND GENEALOGY
      DIVISION. (ROOM 315–S)   *161*

XIII THE SOUTH STAIRWAY. SECOND FLOOR SOUTH   *165*

XIV   THE TRUSTEES' ROOM   *171*

XV   THE SOUTH STAIRWAY TO ASTOR HALL   *187*

XVI   THE 42ND STREET ENTRANCE. THE JEWISH DIVISION. ROOM 80   *191*

XVII THE 42ND STREET STAIRCASE   *199*

XVIII THE WEST FACADE. BRYANT PARK. SOUTH FACADE   *205*

      IDENTIFICATIONS   *217*

      COMPARISON OF ORDERS   *263*

      ILLUSTRATED GLOSSARY OF ARCHITECTURAL AND DECORATIVE TERMS   *265*

      APPENDICES   *275*
      I Building Statistics of the Main Research Library   *275*
      II List of the Varieties of Stone Found in the New York Public Library   *276*
      III Major Donors to the Library as Listed in Astor Hall   *278*
      IV Members of the Library Staff Who Served in World Wars I and II   *279*
      V Founding Life Conservators and Life Conservators   *281*

      FLOOR PLANS   *283*

      INDEX   *289*

FOREWORD

"ONE CANNOT IMAGINE NEW YORK without it—its presence is that of some great natural fact." Thus comments Henry Hope Reed, president of Classical America and author of this volume, in his description of one of the nation's most prized classical buildings, the New York Public Library.

Completed in 1911, after being under construction for ten years, it was typical of America's vision of itself at the turn of the century, a period in American architecture often described as the American Renaissance. The classical style was then the main artistic current of Western Civilization and inspired the sister arts to embellish and enrich all aspects of these structures with sculpture, murals, bronze work, wood carving, and plaster relief. Architects gloried in this tradition, and nowhere more so than in our public libraries.

The idea of having a public library captured the imagination of the American people, and the New York Public Library building is the embodiment of this enthusiasm. Cities, towns, and villages throughout the nation also responded, and libraries built in the classical tradition arose everywhere, including on university campuses.

The magnificent New York Public Library, located in the very heart of New York City, on Fifth Avenue, occupies the entire east side of Bryant Park. The architectural firm of Carrère & Hastings, inspired by the great classical buildings in Paris and Rome, created an edifice of stunning quality—a people's palace of triumphant glory. The building's Corinthian columns, the lion masks of the main facade, the two great urns on the entrance steps, along with the renowned lions on the terrace, firmly establish the sense of grandeur that visitors carry with them as they move into the interior of the structure.

Astor Hall, at the entrance, with its unique stone vault above an awesome white marble interior, sets the tone for the architectural delights that lie in store for the visitor. Sumptuous light brackets, elaborately decorated ceilings, the great gallery extending along the north-south axis of the building on the first floor, the window bays, the doorways, the great stairways, all combine to lift the human spirit and dignify man's achievements. The elaborately decorated Main Reading Room, almost two city blocks in length, located at the top of the building for light and quiet, is a fitting climax to all that the architects wished to achieve.

This book is intended to heighten the appreciation of this landmark by appropriately illuminating its vast splendor and focusing the attention of our citizens once again on the beauty and glory of one of the great Beaux Arts buildings of our time, adding further to civic pride, as the founders of this institution had hoped it would, and celebrating the treasure of mankind's knowledge with which this institution is endowed.

New York City   ARTHUR ROSS
June 1985

ACKNOWLEDGMENTS

THE AUTHOR IS VERY GRATEFUL for assistance extended by the following: Angela Giral, librarian, Christina Huemer, deputy librarian, Herbert Mitchell, bibliographer, and Janet Parks, curator of drawings, Avery Library, Columbia University; Fred Jacobs, superintendant, Frick Collection; Xavier Verstraaten and David Pickman, photograph assistants; David Wright, archivist, Morgan Library; Thomas Barbour, descendant of John Merven Carrère; Paul Marx, Harvard University; Dick Schuler, photographer; Arthur Ward, P. E. Guerin, Inc.; Timothy G. Riordan, wood worker, and James Parker, curator, European Sculpture and Decorative Arts, Metropolitan Museum of Art, John Blatteau, architect; Ethel L. Robinson, Head of Main Library, Cleveland Public Library; Arlene Palmer, Curator, Local History, New Britain Public Library; Jack S. Vaniman, Director, Sales Administration, Schnadig Corporation; Kevin Voll, President, Risom Marble Corporation.

Two doctoral theses were useful: Channing Blake's *Carrère & Hastings* and, particularly, Dr. Jean-Pierre Isbouts' *Carrère & Hastings, Architects of an Era*.

At every step the author was helped by members of the staff of the Central Research Library of the New York Public Library. Among those were of special assistance were: President Vartan Gregorian, Vice-President Gregory Long, Assistant Secretary of the corporation Bridie Race, and Coordinator of Exhibitions Diantha D. Schull; in the public Relations Office, Manager Betsy Pinover, staff members Helen Morris and Alberta Green, and former members Joyce Yaeger, Lauren Howard, Jeffrey Hon, and Debby Nadler; in the Map Division, Chief Alice C. Hudson and Assistant Chief Robert B. Sperling; in the United States History, Local History and Genealogy Division, Chief Gunther E. Pohl and First Assistant Barbara Hillman;

in the Berg Collection, Curator Lola L. Szladits; in the Art, Prints and Photographs Division Assistants Anthony Cardillo, David B. Combs, Sharon Frost, Harriet Burdock, and Jerry Romero; in the Public Services Division, Assistant Chief of the Main Reading Room Section, Elizabeth Diefendorf; in the Office of Special Collections, Director Donald Anderle, with his staff Curator of the Brooke Russell Astor Room for Rare Books and Manuscripts William L. Joyce, and Assistants in Archives Melanie Yolles and John Stinson; in the Graphics Office, Coordinator Marilan Lund; in the Photographic Services Division, Chief Michael Calvano and Assistant Chief Rocco Lombardo; in Facilities Operations, Manager Fred T. Catapano, Security Section Officers Nathaniel Bell and Robert P. Quarg, and former business manager Jerry Gold.

THE NEW YORK PUBLIC LIBRARY

ITS ARCHITECTURE AND DECORATION

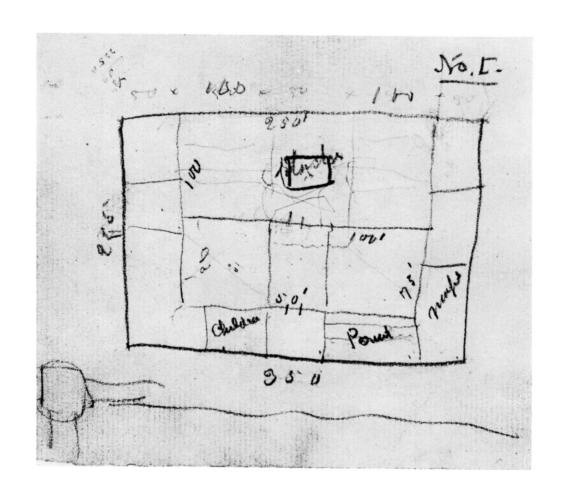

INTRODUCTION

THE NEW YORK PUBLIC LIBRARY, with its Main Research Library and its many branches, is very much part of the city. In fact, it is impossible to think of New York without it. This is especially true of the great building on Fifth Avenue, between 40th and 42nd Streets, whose presence is that of some great natural fact. It would appear to have always been there. For that reason, for the purpose of this book, *the* Library is the magnificent structure. Visibly, you might say triumphantly, it is the city's great treasure house and resource.*

It is not easy to grasp that the institution, with its association with the building, has a history. However thin its past may have been, the institution reaches back a century and a half. The clue is on the front of the building. There, on the attic wall over the central portico between freestanding statues, are incised inscriptions bearing the names, reading from left to right, John Jacob Astor, James Lenox, and Samuel Jones Tilden.

OPPOSITE. *John Shaw Billings' sketch of the plan for the first floor of the Library, 1897. Courtesy Rare Book and Manuscript Division, The New York Public Library, Astor, Lenox and Tilden Foundations.*

* For all the importance of the New York Public Library, its Main Research Library building went into partial eclipse beginning in the 1930s, with the shift in fashion in the arts away from the classical tradition. Therefore, it was something of a novelty when Classical America, the society founded to encourage the classical tradition in the arts of this country, obtained permission to sponsor a Sunday visit to the building in 1972. Leading the tour were the late John Barrington Bayley, designer of the new wing of the Frick Collection and the first president of Classical America, and the author. The visit's success resulted in several more sponsored by the society and in the Library's instituting the program of weekly tours of the building that are now so popular. Much as it prompted the Library's tours, the 1972 visit is at the origin of this book.

At least one, John Jacob Astor (1763–1848), is known, so closely is his name bound to the history of the city and of the nation. He came to this country from Walldorf, in Germany, and lived to make his immense fortune in New York. A fur merchant, a shipowner, a financier who helped our country in the War of 1812, and, lastly, an investor in city real estate, he became the nation's richest man by the 1830s. With what might be called enforced leisure, he turned in his later years to things literary, drawing about him poets and writers. He commissioned Washington Irving to write the story of Astoria, the ill-fated trading post in Oregon. The poet Fitz-Greene Halleck was his secretary. And there was his friendship with the scholar Joseph Green Cogswell.

With Astor's literary interest came the collecting of books. Beginning in the 1830s, he began to buy and he turned to Cogswell for counsel and help. He gathered so many books that Cogswell put forward the vision of a great *public* library for the city; Cogswell even threatened to leave when Astor wavered on the project. Astor was like many wealthy men who, in retirement, are not quite certain where to channel their interests; he needed someone of Cogswell's strength and clear sense of purpose to make the project a reality. The result was that Astor, on his death, left both his library and funds to house it in a proper building. Occupying what is now the seat of the Shakespeare Theater, on Lafayette Street, the Astor Library opened in 1852 with Cogswell as librarian.

The Lenox name is familiar, at least to New Yorkers, because of Lenox Avenue, north of Central Park, and of Lenox Hill Hospital, on Park Avenue, but very few know anything of the man who bore it. James Lenox (1800–1880), a graduate of Columbia College in 1818, inherited a family-owned importing firm and extensive properties mainly in the East 70s of Manhattan. He was a bibliophile with some of the eccentricities of the collector. So big was his collection of books that in 1870 he built the Lenox Library on Fifth Avenue between 70th and 71st Streets, on the site of the Frick Collection. (The architect of the building was Richard Morris Hunt, whose memorial stands directly across from the Frick Collection, in the wall of Central Park.) The library was reserved primarily for scholars.

Samuel Jones Tilden (1814–1886) was a very successful railroad attorney at a time when railroads were important. He turned to politics, becoming governor of New York (1875–1877) and, in 1876, the Democratic candidate for the presidency, but he lost to Rutherford B. Hayes. Tilden's town house, on the south side of Gramercy Park, is now the National Arts Club. When Tilden died he left approximately $5 million to found a free public library. Unfortunately, relatives, who had been left out of the will, sued and succeeded in breaking it. In 1891, when the will was settled out of court, only $2 million was left for his library.

It must not be imagined that at the time of Tilden's death two large, flourishing libraries existed in the city. The one set up by Astor was showing signs of age in every way, largely because the Astor descendants had lost interest in it. The Lenox Library, despite its usefulness, especially in American history, had deteriorated after the founder's death. The Tilden bequest was to give the impulse for a new library combining the two. The key factor of the Tilden bequest, and this was as important as the money, was the presence of several trustees of the estate who were determined that the city have one great library. Andrew Haswell Green, the Tilden partner who had such an important role in the development of Central Park in its early years, was one of them. So was John Bigelow, onetime editor and owner of *The Evening Post,* predecessor of today's *New York Post,* and General Consul and American Minister to France in the 1860s. Although several others had first suggested it, he was to be the prime mover in the consolidation of the libraries and in the selection of the library site. In those days, the site was covered by the distributing reservoir of the Croton Aqueduct System (the receiving reservoirs were in Central Park). Bigelow went so far as to publish an article in *Scribner's Magazine* with plans and elevations by Ernest Flagg, who was to be the architect of the United States Naval Academy, calling for a building on the site.

The Distributing Reservoir of the Croton Aqueduct System built in 1845. View to the northwest from the corner of Fifth Avenue and 40th Street. Courtesy Museum of the City of New York.

Bigelow saw that, with the reduction of the Tilden funds, a new worthwhile library would come about only by merging the two existing libraries. His strong allies in this were Wall Street lawyers. He had Lewis Cass Ledyard of Carter & Ledyard, which today is Carter Ledyard & Milburn, join the Tilden board. As it turned out, Ledyard had a close friend on the Astor board, John L. Cadwalader of Cadwalder & Strong (the Strong being of the family of George Templeton Strong, the diarist, the firm later becoming Cadwalader, Wickersham & Taft). Cadwalader had thought of a possible merger with the Tilden Trust. Then John Stewart Kennedy, the president of the Lenox board, heard of the proposal and saw a place for his library. The man who came to represent the Lenox in the eventual negotiations was George Lockhart Rives, of Olin & Rives, Wall Street lawyer.

The three lawyers drafted the consolidation agreement, which was signed May 23, 1895, in the form of a new corporation, "The New York Public Library, Astor, Lenox and Tilden Foundations," organized to "establish and maintain a free public library and reading-room in the City of New York . . ." Subsequently, the branch system, made up of existing neighborhood libraries, was added, along with a gift of $1 million from Andrew Carnegie.

The next momentous step came on December 11, with the naming of a director, Dr. John Shaw Billings. If John Jacob Astor was more than well served by Joseph Green Cogswell, the City of New York had an even better servant in Dr. Billings. He, more than any other person, shaped the institution and *the building* we have today.

Billings was born in 1838 on a farm in southern Indiana, not far from Cincinnati. An omnivorous reader with an excellent memory, the young Billings went to Miami University in Oxford, Ohio, and to Miami Medical College, from which he graduated in 1858. In the spring of 1862, he joined the Union Army as first lieutenant and assistant surgeon. After duty in military hospitals, he was posted to the Virginia front. He was at Gettysburg, and after a brief spell in New York during the Draft Riots, he went back to northern Virginia with the Army of the Potomac. In 1864, he was assigned to the Surgeon General's Office in the War Department. It was here that, after the war, he began his great work in medical bibliography, with an *Index Catalogue* and an *Index Medicus* of current medical literature. These were to bring him fame, actually more abroad than at home. Added to this labor was that of surveying and inspecting for government departments and advising on hospital design. In 1875, for example, his plan for the Johns Hopkins Hospital in Baltimore was the one chosen. Billings also found time to write a history of American medicine. And he was in charge of collecting vital and medical statistics for the 1880 and 1890 censuses. After his time in Washington, he went to Philadelphia to be Professor of Hygiene and Director of the University Hospital of the University of Pennsylvania. His friend, John Cadwalader, brought him to the attention of his fellow trustees, and Billings was named Library Director on December 11, 1895.

One of his first responsibilities was to help in obtaining the reservoir site. After overcoming opposition and conflicts, Billings and the trustees were able, in 1897, to get the state legislature to pass a bill authorizing the city to raze the reservoir.

The next order of business was the planning of the Library building. Billings drew the basic plan, which shows a first floor 350 by 225 feet, with two inner courtyards 100 by 75 feet, and a stack room 250 by 100 feet. Between the courtyards is a space 75 by 50 feet. Several of the spaces are identified: "Stacks," "children," "period,"

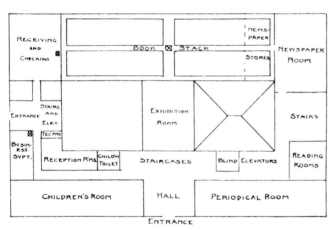

First Floor

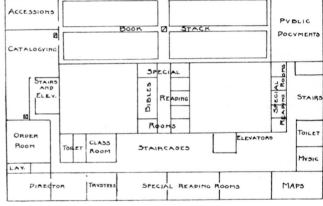

Second Floor

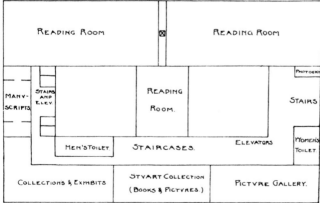

Third Floor

Plans for the Library's three floors, based on John Shaw Billings' ideas. They were part of the first competition, 1897. Courtesy President's Office, The New York Public Library, Astor, Lenox and Tilden Foundations.

"maps." From this were developed the plans for the two competitions in which the architect was chosen.

In addition, Billings specified that there be a monumental reading room on the top floor, directly above the stacks. This was his grand concept. He was determined that the reader have a well-lighted, airy room, removed from the city's noise, that would be cool in summer and, not least, that would have no columns, even for so large a space.

The jury for the first competition, in addition to Billings, consisted of Professor William R. Ware, head of the School of Architecture at Columbia University and author of *The American Vignola,* a basic text for instruction in classical architecture (part of the Classical America Series in Art and Architecture), and Bernard R. Green, the engineer who had so important a role in the design and construction of the Library of Congress (see Herbert Small, *The Library of Congress: Its Architecture and Decoration* also in the Series). From the eighty-eight designs submitted, twelve were chosen. For the second competition, six leading firms, including McKim, Mead & White and Carrère & Hastings, were invited to compete, making a total of eighteen plans.

On November 10, 1897, the winners of the competition were chosen: McKim, Mead & White came in third, Howard & Cauldwell (selected from the first competition) came in second, and Carrère & Hastings took first place. McKim, Mead & White, for some reason, did not abide by the plan submitted by the trustees; although adhering to the general scheme, the firm boldly offered variations. The second scheme was put aside because Howard & Cauldwell, despite presenting a strong design, failed to pay due attention to the library functions.

It is interesting to compare the three submissions, particularly in their treatment of the main facade. In McKim, Mead & White's plan, it is impossible not to notice a certain sobriety, almost plainness, despite the presence of a Corinthian order and flaming urns on the attic. What are wholly absent are points of emphasis. For example, only the flight of steps distinguishes the entrance door from the windows. There is no accent to the roof line. At the building's south and north ends there are no pavilions or pediments.

As for Howard & Cauldwell's facade, it is very close to the winning design. The main differences lie in the first-floor plans. Key variances are to be seen in the handling of the vestibule, now called Astor Hall, and in the long south-north corridor next to it. Carrère & Hastings triumphed in combining the vestibule with the two flights of stairs, which their competitor had placed in a separate stairway

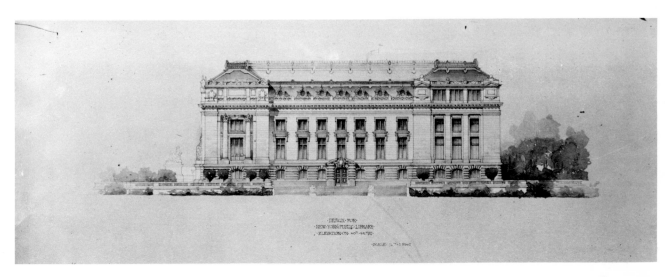

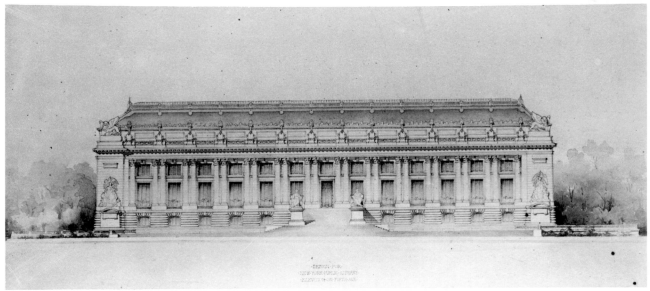

hall. In so doing, the winner gave a dimension and depth to Astor Hall, obtaining perspectives and penetrations absent in the other. They also obtained a wider and longer south-north gallery, which extended the building's length, thus permitting a vista rarely found in American architecture.

In the same way, by combining room and stairway to achieve a large space, Carrère & Hastings secured the splendid third floor landing, adding a portion of a south-north corridor to room and stairway. And by linking the three, they made possible the high windows overlooking the courtyards. This comparison underscores the high

The design of McKim, Mead & White for the Fifth Avenue facade. Courtesy Museum of the City of New York.

Howard & Cauldwell's design for the Library. The Fifth Avenue elevation

Howard & Cauldwell's design for the Library. The rear or Bryant Park elevation

quality of the submissions, and it also shows the trustees' wisdom in choosing the design of Carrère & Hastings.

Thomas Hastings offers the best explanation for the firm's design of the facade:

In the study of the exterior of the Library the main object has been to express in facade the interior arrangement of the building. The three main arches, or entrances, running through two stories, show in facade the main entrance hall, or staircase hall. The large pediments showing above the roofs, are designed distinctly to express the fact that in this portion of the building are the main reading rooms. The attic story over the main cornice, without windows, but lighted by skylights on the roof, contains the Stuart collection, picture galleries and other exhibits [now the Edna B. Salomon Room]. The series of arches (very large in scale) to either side of the entrances on the first story express two large rooms in this portion of the building; one for the children's reading rooms [now the Map Division] and the other for the periodical room [now the DeWitt Wallace Periodical Room].

The facade of the building is set back about ninety feet from the street building line, and all of the terraces, or fountains at either end.

It has been the desire of all those connected with Library to have a simple and dignified design, not depending on an over amount of ornamentation, Renaissance in style, based on classic principles, and modern in character.

No description better explains the approach of Carrère & Hastings. That "the exterior of the building" was so designed as "to express in facade the interior arrangement," was at the heart of their training at the Ecole des Beaux Arts in Paris. The plan dominated and had to be "expressed" on the exterior. (By way of contrast, what might be termed the more traditional classical approach is one in

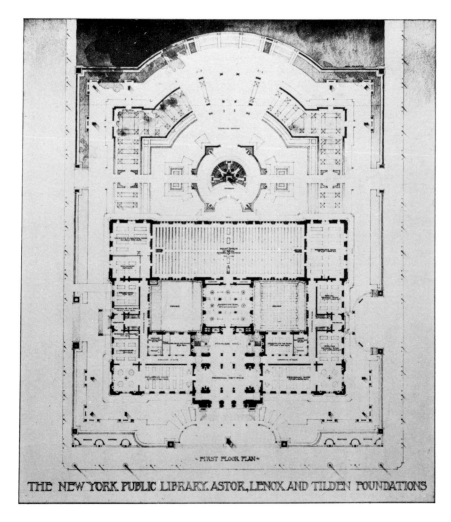

Howard & Cauldwell's design for the Library

1 2

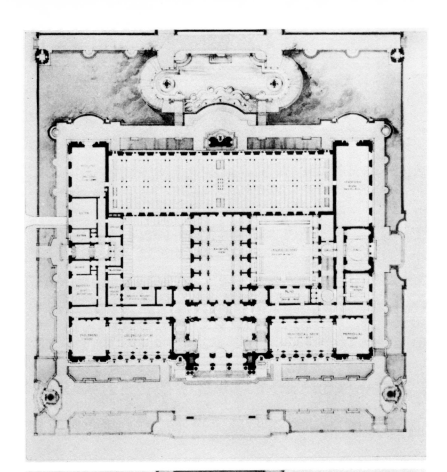

The winning design of Carrère & Hastings

OPPOSITE, ABOVE. *Fifth Avenue elevation*
MIDDLE. *42nd Street elevation*
Rear or Bryant Park elevation

First floor plan

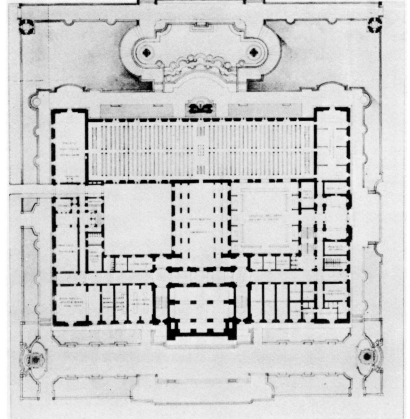

Third floor plan

which the facade, while not divorced from the plan, is a distinct element to itself.) What is extraordinary about the building is that, despite what has been called the "dictatorship of the plan," the building is throughout such a reward to the eye.

If there was any sign of contemporary French influence in the elevation, it was to be found in the massing and the tripartite division of the main facade. Here the influence stemmed not from existing French buildings, but in the teaching of the Ecole, which shaped the prize-winning designs of the school's competitions, especially for the Grand Prix de Rome, the prize that entitled the winner to a long residence in the French Academy in Rome. In fact, in 1898, *The Architectural Record* published without comment the facade of a Grand Prix design that, in part, resembled that of Carrère & Hastings.

Such comparisons were part of the times. As we go about the building, we will see less evidence of the Ecole and more of the French classical. The use of so much stone on the inside of the building (the stone vault of Astor Hall is a good example), the detail of the door plates, possibly the form of the balusters of the terrace, the Ls back to back at the main entrance—these and other elements will be noted in this book. They are, however, so mixed with a general interpretation of the classical that they have a special quality of their own.

Hardly had Carrère & Hastings been designated the building's architects than they made changes in the elevations. The most important of these was adopting the Corinthian instead of the Ionic for the exterior order. On the Fifth Avenue front, what had been pilasters became fluted engaged columns. Where there had been pairs of columns on the sides of the central porch there were now walls, and the porch's attic was raised. They made the Main Reading Room

higher. Minor changes, such as the disappearance of the columns at the south and north ends of the terrace, also took place. Most important was setting the windows in two-story high bays on the 42nd and 40th street sides.

Changes continued as the architects had time to make them what with the removal of the distributing reservoir not beginning until June 1899. There was a tendency to reduce the ornament on all the facades. The acroterion at the peak of the main gable disappeared. On the west front overlooking Bryant Park, a pair of massive rostra that stood at either end at the top of the Main Reading Room wall were taken out. Visually, the most important step was the realigning of the narrow vertical shafts of the stack windows of the west front. In the original design, they had occurred in alternating singles and pairs; now the shafts were widened to admit more light and were placed across the facade equidistant from each other. Another change involved the placing of the William Cullen Bryant monument with its bronze statue of the poet. At first it abutted the west facade; it was given its present site several feet forward from the wall, still remaining part of the terrace that encompasses the building.

While the design underwent changes, the trustees came to a decision on the material for the exterior. John Shaw Billings had wanted brick, but the trustees leaned toward Indiana limestone, as mentioned in the final competition. Their choice was a natural one. Limestone, which had first been brought to the city by the architect Richard Morris Hunt for the William Kissam Vanderbilt mansion (formerly at the northwest corner of Fifth Avenue and 52nd Street) had become the city's premier building stone, succeeding brownstone. But the architects rejected it for white marble, which was easy

Photograph of the model that has later changes such as the disappearance of the acroterion from the peak of the main gable.

to carve and which, while sharply bright at first, would with time have a pearly gray quality.

Specifying white marble was simple enough. The problem was where to find it with the right color and with uniform color and texture, and to find it in sufficient quantity. The sheer amount used at the Library must be emphasized. The exterior marble has an average depth of twelve inches, as does the revetment of the piers in Astor Hall. While there are New York buildings with large blocks of white marble such as the kind seen at Federal Hall Memorial (the former Subtreasury Building and Custom House) on Wall Street and the Morgan Library on 36th Street off Madison Avenue (in both buildings the joints have no mortar), neither equals the Library in the sheer quantity employed. About 530,000 cubic feet went into the building compared to the 25,000 cubic feet at the New York Chamber of Commerce on Liberty Street and 50,000 cubic feet for the New York Stock Exchange.

The marble singled out was found in two quarries on Dorset Mountain, near Danby and Dorset close by Manchester, Vermont. Sixty-five percent of the stone quarried was rejected, as not fitting the architects' determination to obtain the best. (The rejected stone was not wasted; it simply found its way into other buildings such as that of the Harvard Medical School.)

Although they had found the desired marble, Carrère & Hastings did not attempt the ambitious device of having the shafts of the exterior columns monoliths, that is to say, of one piece, although monolithic shafts are to be found inside the building. Instead, they had the shafts made of drums of the same height as the course blocks of the wall. There is a certain fascination for the eye in following the horizontal of the courses, the drums, and the mortar joints.

It should be pointed out that the foot-thick marble is set against load-bearing walls of solid brick four feet thick. There are no steel posts in the building, only steel girders. The foot-thick revetment of marble is extraordinary for so large a building; in most cases stone facing is made of thin panels. Interestingly, at the Frick Collection, also designed by Carrère & Hastings, the stone, an Indiana limestone, is laid in courses alternatively 8 inches and 4 inches thick.

Construction techniques need not deter us, because they are as unimportant an aspect of the New York Public Library as they are for most great buildings in the world. To write the history of architecture or to describe the making of a building in engineering terms is much like writing the history of Venetian architecture in the vocabulary of pile driving or describing the career of a painter with a lengthy discussion of the making of canvas. What counts is the style and how it shaped the building we see.

The New York Public Library is classical, as were most of the important buildings constructed at the turn of the century. It is hard for us today to grasp the fact that in those days the United States was, at least in architecture, the great classical country, because the tradition has largely vanished in the arts today. By the 1890s, this nation had become the chief heir to the tradition that is the main artistic current of Western civilization. The classical dominated the visible American world and, if it was largely absent from painting and sculpture, it was still very much part of decoration— be it architectural sculpture, plaster work, bronze work, wrought iron, and the other crafts that contribute so much to a classical building.

What is the classical? The definition used by the organization Classical America, a sponsor of this book, and based on that of the artist Pierce Rice, is the generalized and idealized interpretation of nature begun by the Greeks and the Romans and continued in the Renaissance. Such was the force of the classical at the turn of the century that it never died in this country surviving, as it has, in architecture and interior decoration.

Central to the Western tradition is the importance given the human figure. In the art of no other civilization does it have the chief role as it does in the art of the West. Pierce Rice in his forthcoming *Man As Hero: The Human Figure in Western Art* has pointed out that the archetype of the idealized and generalized part of the human body is the Greek female profile, an ever-recurring image, even in our own time. The treatment of the classical figure is seen in the outline of the profile applied to the whole body. In this way, says Rice, "we are offered . . . a kind of synthesized view of nature. The continuity of the arm is emphasized, not its interruption by elbow and wrist. . . . The limbs and heads themselves are subordinated to the unity of the body itself." The result is "the ennoblement of the human figure."

More than any of the human figures, the baby, according to Rice, symbolizes the art of the West. It is wonderful to see this figure, even the baby with wings, or, the cherub, which is so much a part of the decoration of the Library. There are, in addition, any number of winged figures and a variety of masks. All this ornament, like the detail of the towers of classical skyscrapers, goes unnoticed.

The generalized and idealized treatment extends to an array of beasts, real and mythical. The classical artist draws on the animal kingdom as often as he draws on the human, if not more so. The visitor can go about the building counting lion masks, lion paws, dolphins, and variations on the eagle and the griffon.

If that is insufficient, flora abounds. Here the great generalized and idealized form is that of the common Mediterranean plants, *Acanthus mollis* and *Acanthus spinosus,* commonly known as Bear's Britches. It has been a source of classical enrichment for centuries, one that achieves its most splendid shape in the Corinthian and Composite capitals. For this reason it is almost as symbolic of the tradition as the cherub. For some architects, such as John Barrington Bayley, the acanthus is the morphological symbol of Western civilization, much as the chrysanthemum is that of the Japanese or the lotus that of the ancient Egyptians.

The enrichment is hardly confined to the acanthus. Some of the more common decorative motifs are the egg-and-dart, the leaf-and-dart, pearls, and bead-and-reel. And there are the several plain treatments of surfaces in the form of moldings with such names as cyma recta, cyma reversa, ovolo, and cavetto. They are defined and illustrated in the Glossary in this book.

John Merven Carrère and Thomas Hastings gathered all of this heritage as they went about designing the Library. It was not enough that the building had to stand up, that it had to serve as a giant warehouse for printed matter, manuscripts, and incunabula and that it had to meet the needs of a large reading public. The building had to be a monument, a triumphant adornment to the city, *the people's palace* to assuage the visual hunger of local pride.

The challenge was accepted by the two architects. Beyond the planning and the engineering, beyond providing the many facilities, they had to design rooms, halls, stairs, alcoves, and other appurtenances having the right proportion, scale, balance, and symmetry. Major public rooms had to meet the aesthetic demands of the human eye. Ornaments had to be selected and skillfully adapted to fit a vault, a wall, and an attic. A floor had to be given a pattern.

Tradition was by no means limited to ornament. Central to the design philosophy of the classical architect is the attaining of correct proportion and scale. There is only one way of gaining command of both: the study of the five orders, namely Tuscan, Doric, Ionic, Corinthian, and Composite. By drawing and drafting them and constantly studying them, the classical architect can attain his end. Proportion is the relation of parts to each other and the relation of the individual part to the whole. The best example is the human figure. If a man has abnormally large feet or hands, they are said to be out of proportion to the rest of his body. If he is a very short and yet perfectly proportioned, he is out of scale. Six feet is the standard

ABOVE. *The Portico of the New York Library*

RIGHT. *"Navigation," one of the four ures on the Terrace flagpole bases*

LEFT. *The Library's familiar lion*

ABOVE LEFT. *A doorway at the main entrance at Astor Hall*

ABOVE RIGHT. *Columns, arches and a candelabrum in Astor Hall*

LEFT. *A ceiling in the South-North Gallery off Astor Hall*

ABOVE LEFT. *Astor Hall with its marble vault, seen from the South Stairway*

ABOVE RIGHT. *Looking west from Astor Hall to the South-North Gallery and beyond*

RIGHT. *Enriched coffering on a ceiling in the South-North Gallery off Astor Hall*

The bronze door to the Gottesman Exhibition Hall

The Gottesman Exhibition Hall

A panel in the wood ceiling of the Gottesman Exhibition Hall

The Gottesman Exhibition Hall

OPPOSITE, ABOVE RIGHT. *Open work of the bronze door at the south end of the South-North Gallery*

OPPOSITE, ABOVE LEFT. *A semidome in the ceiling of the DeWitt Wallace Periodical Room*

OPPOSITE, BELOW LEFT. *The marble railing of the South Stairway in Astor Hall*

OPPOSITE, BELOW RIGHT. *The doorway to the Main Reading Room*

ABOVE LEFT. *Cherubs and a scroll cartouche on the Main Reading Room ceiling*

ABOVE RIGHT. *Winged figures on the Main Reading Room ceiling*

BELOW LEFT. *Coffers with rosettes and a vine band on the Main Reading Room ceiling with the modillion cornice of the wall*

BELOW RIGHT. *A coffer in the Main Reading Room ceiling with foliated Vitruvian scrolls and a vine band*

OVERLEAF. *The south half of the Main Reading Room*

height for measuring human scale. In sculpture, the human scale is termed life-size; anything larger is heroic, the very large being colossal, as the Statue of Liberty. In architecture, there is human scale and the monumental, with the very large being the colossal. Proportion and scale for the architect are defined by the column, which is divided into base, shaft, and capital. The width of the shaft at its base fixes the module. The height of the shafts is seven times its diameter in the Tuscan, eight times in the Doric, nine times in the Ionic, and ten times in the Corinthian and the Composite. Within these proportions are variations but they are never too great, for the result will be ugly. These modules are applied to the design of a doorway, a wall, a window, any part of the building. (For the best treatment of the subject, see William R. Ware, *The American Vignola,* in this Series.)

Today, in the age of the "Free Spirit" in the arts, we may smile at the rules and strictures of the tradition. The smile soon disappears on seeing the work of those who, attempting the classical, have not accepted them. Take the column as the most obvious example. If the capital is too small in relation to the shaft, if the height of the shaft is not in proper relation to its diameter, if there is too much or too little entasis in the shaft, or if the channeling of a fluted shaft is crude, it will be only too obvious that the work is the product of ignorance or of an architect wholly lacking in skill. The classical in the arts, even at a mundane level, is not easily achieved. It is the product of thorough training, skill and experience, these qualities and others with which Carrère and Hastings were endowed.

The classical tradition had existed in this country almost from the time of the first settlements. The style was present even during the Civil War, but for all the affection we lavish on the buildings of that generation it can only be called quaint. The dramatic change occurred in the 1880s, with the design of the William Kissam Vanderbilt mansion by Richard Morris Hunt. This building was unrivaled in opulence and quality and was, as well, the first in New York City to be built of Indiana limestone. Others followed. The Villard houses, of brownstone, are part of the change. Standing behind St. Patrick's Cathedral, on Madison Avenue, and built according to the designs of Joseph Morrill Wells of McKim, Mead & White, they brought a new dimension to American architecture by looking to Rome, as well as Paris, for inspiration. At the start, the new architecture of opulence was limited to mansions but it was soon to be seen in state capitols, banks, hotels, courthouses, churches, college buildings, and, by no means least, libraries.

Into a setting that was becoming more and more splendid stepped two young men, John Merven Carrère and Thomas Hastings. Car-

The Carrère family, with John Merven Carrère on the far left. Courtesy Thomas Barbour.

John Merven Carrère in middle age. Courtesy Thomas Barbour.

rère, born in Rio de Janeiro in 1858 of a Baltimore family of French descent, had gone to school in Switzerland and then studied architecture at the Ecole des Beaux Arts in Paris. Thomas Hastings was a New Yorker, born in 1860, the son of the Reverend Thomas Hastings, a Presbyterian minister who became president of the Union Theological Seminary. (His grandfather, also Thomas Hastings, wrote hymns and was a well-known composer in his time.) After Columbia College the young Hastings, too, went to the Ecole des Beaux Arts.

The Ecole Nationale Supérieure des Beaux Arts, it must be remembered, was the great training school in the arts in the last century for Americans. Richard Morris Hunt was the first American to study architecture there, in the 1850s. By the 1880s, Americans formed the largest foreign contingent in the architecture ateliers. Carrère, at the school from 1878 to 1882, was in several ateliers, the best known of which was that of Léon Ginain. Hastings was there from 1880 to 1882 in the Atelier Pierre André.

The work involved drawing and drafting under the *maître,* master of the atelier, who was informally known as the *patron,* boss. The *patron,* who was a successful practicing architect, visited the atelier several times a week as critic. The skills, however, were acquired by learning from fellow students. Advancement came on the basis of competitions. (The highest of them, open only to French citizens, was for the Grand Prix de Rome, which entitled the winner to become a fellow at the French Academy in Rome. Mention of this competition simply underscores the importance of the Roman classical at the school.) While eclectic in the matter of style, for students worked even in the Gothic and the Romanesque, the core of the instruction was the classical, from the drawing and the drafting of the Five Orders to the study of great classical buildings and monuments. Out of this came an understanding of proportion and scale, an awareness of the role of ornament, and all the essentials that contribute to the success of a design. Beyond the walls of the Ecole were the great works of the past from Paris to Rome, to be studied and drawn.

Thomas Hastings in middle age. Drawing by Henri Royar. Courtesy The New York Public Library, Astor, Lenox and Tilden Foundations.

Perhaps what best demonstrates the range of the training of the Ecole was the fact that, with its more important competitions, the students had to design a great building or monument. The building might be an embassy, an opera house, the main center of a spa, or a large memorial; it was always something on a palatial scale. The result was that when Carrère and Hastings returned from Paris, they could not have been better equipped to design a great public building, a people's palace.

The two architects met briefly at the Ecole des Beaux Arts, but their friendship and association began when they met again as draftsmen in the office of McKim, Mead & White, the other great nursery of architects in that era. They were there only two years or so when they founded their partnership, in 1885.

The spark for the new firm was a commission to design the Ponce de Leon Hotel in St. Augustine, Florida, for Henry Morrison Flagler, a friend of the Hastings' father. It was to be the first of a number of commissions from Flagler, a member of the Standard Oil Trust, who was investing large sums in the development of the Florida East Coast Railroad. As the railroad advanced south so did the Florida commissions; one of them was to be Flagler's Palm Beach mansion, "Whitehall," now a museum.

What was to be remarked about the firm's work—and it was true of most of the Paris Men, as they were known—was how little it reflected contemporary French architecture. Admittedly the American architect obtained commissions for building types that did not exist in Europe, such as the skyscraper, college buildings on a campus, and the public library. In no other nation does the public library building occupy so important a place and status, as in the American city, town, and suburb. Often as not, it is the community's chief ornament, and if not the main one it ranks with the best, whether in Detroit, Boston, San Francisco, or Philadelphia, or in Lafayette, Indiana, and Winona, Minnesota. No matter the building type, the Americans struck out on their own, working in the classical style and giving the tradition a new dimension. The product was American Classical. In their work, Carrère and Hastings had complete mastery of the idiom, and nowhere is this more true than in the New York Public Library.

We have mentioned that the French influence did exist, not in architecture but in painting and sculpture. In the handling of the subject, notably the figure, the treatment was realistic, or "Naturalistic." The prime examples of this Naturalism, a product of nineteenth-century France, are the figures by Frederick MacMonnies, on either side of the Library's Fifth Avenue porch and the pediment sculpture by George Grey Barnard, at the south and north ends of the main facade. It is also to be seen, although faintly, in the female figures in relief in the bronze doors of the 42nd Street entrance. Elsewhere throughout the building the handling of the figure, or parts thereof, is classical. And that applies as well for the several beasts, such as the lion masks and the dolphins and it is also reflected in the plant detail. What had taken place was that the artist-sculptor, attuned to the shift to Naturalism, had turned to realism, whereas the sculptor and modeller of architectural ornament, whether in stone, wood, stucco, or bronze, had remained classical. The artisans studied the antique or work derived from the antique, that is, ancient Rome chiefly, while the artist-sculptor had rejected the antique for the live model.

Whether craftsmen or draftsmen, they formed an army of classically trained skills of an unusually high order. The architect William Adams Delano, future partner in the firm of Delano & Aldrich, began his career in Carrère & Hastings in the 1890s; he recalled that, at the time, most of the draftsmen were products of the Ecole des Beaux Arts. Carrère & Hastings as did McKim, Mead & White, served as way station for the returning Paris Men before they practiced on their own. Besides Delano, there was Chester Aldrich, his partner, Welles Bosworth, architect of the main campus of the Massachusetts Institute of Technology, and Donn Barber, designer of the former Cotton Exchange on Hanover Square. Even the draftsmen who came out of the few American architectural schools and technical institutes had a command of drafting and drawing unknown today.

Nor were Carrère and Hastings afraid of books any more than others in the profession. Architects in those days had large office libraries, and their staff was encouraged to make full use of them. Readers in the Library will see books with the bookplates of Thomas Hastings. On his death in 1929, his widow gave 1,500 volumes to the Library, along with scrapbooks of engravings and photographs collected over a full professional life.

The books and scrapbooks were an added resource to supplement the memory. The architects and draftsmen would turn to them for designs and ornamental details. There was usually no automatic borrowing unless the design of detail fitted their purpose exactly. They were not going to reinvent the wheel of architecture. If, as in the instance of the exterior capitals, they found one to their purpose, they used it as a guide. Their exemplar was the Corinthian Order of the famous twin buildings on the Place de la Concorde in Paris by Ange-Jacques Gabriel. No doubt there are similar instances among the reliefs in wood or plaster. In classical architecture, much as in sculpture in classical painting sculpture, there is constant resort to the accumulated heritage.

Perhaps the most satisfactory way to outline the firm of Carrère & Hastings is to compare it to one of the big painting studios of the past, such as the one that belonged to Rubens in Antwerp. The seventeenth-century artist would lay out the cartoon for a giant canvas and work with or delegate the work to a squad of trained assistants. A century later, Giovanni Battista Tiepolo, in Venice, had his sons and several assistants help execute his vast frescoes which astonish us today.

Outside the drafting room the firm's partners could turn to the multitude of craftsmen. There were the modelers, not as we understand the term, makers of models of buildings, but makers of plaster models of a capital, a decorative relief, a cornice, or a carved wood panel. The models would serve the stone carvers, the stucco workers, and wood carvers. When the building was under construction, Carrère & Hastings had first a temporary structure, later temporary quarters in the unfinished building, for the modelers along with a place for draftsmen and contractors.

Several modeling firms were in charge: John Lostis, Lostis & Neuman, and Neuman & Even. Little is known of the firms or their men. In 1863, when the modelers founded their guild, the New-York Wood-Carvers and Modelers Association, the members were German and French. The charter of the Association was published in German and French as well as in English, and meetings were often conducted in German. At the turn of the century, the German element remained strong, although there were now American-born and Italian-born members. An example of the care and thoroughness of Carrère and Hastings and their insistence to leave nothing to chance was their making, in 1902, a full-scale model in plaster of two of the bays of the main facade. This was not often done, although the ease of executing such a model had been demonstrated by the plaster buildings of the great expositions of the day, including the one in Buffalo, where the two architects had been in charge.

It has been noted how Carrère and Hastings decided to give up monoliths for the shafts of the exterior columns, replacing them with drums. While they sacrificed ornament, particularly between the lower and upper windows, they had Alexander Phimister Proctor model the lion head, mouthing a ring, that adorns the keystone of the lower window.

Everywhere there is evidence of the architects' attention to every

The modeling room in the unfinished building, with the modelers at work on a Corinthian capital. Courtesy Building Maintenance and Operations Department, The New York Public Library, Astor, Lenox and Tilden Foundations.

part of the building, down to the smallest detail. If they turned to the work of an eighteenth-century French architect for guidance, they called in a contemporary sculptor who was celebrated for his animal sculpture to do a lion's head.

The building cost New York City $9,002,523.09. This was, to be sure, no small sum, but with the skill, plain hard work, and talent forthcoming at all levels, from stone-carver to architect, as well as intense pride in the whole project, the people of New York obtained one of the nation's great monuments.

Of course, for all their efforts, the architects did not gain every desired end. Several of their aims seem particularly ambitious. One might think that once they obtained the commission they would rest,

NOV. 1ST 1902

2 6

temporary, occurred in the spring of 1919. The return of the American Expeditionary Force occasioned parades and celebrations. Part of the city's welcome were the embellishments along Fifth Avenue. Thomas Hastings designed a splendid triumphal arch and columns for the stretch along Madison Square. And for the terrace of the Library he produced magnificent displays of trophies and four assemblages of shields, spears, halberds, and other weapons. Atop each were swags of cloth and eagle-bearing globes. This was decoration in the grand tradition. Nothing, of course, equals the classical in fulfilling the panoply of civic celebration.

The facade of the building remained unchanged. To be sure, Bryant

A giant trophy on the Library terrace in the spring of 1919. Photo by Byron, courtesy Museum of the City of New York.

Park was converted in 1934 from the picturesque to the formal, making it the finest classical park in the country.

A year or two later came several modest changes inside the building. The Berg Collection Room obtained its fine paneling by Eggers & Higgins in 1940, and the Arents Collection, its paneling, designed by Aymar Embury II in 1944. The style of both is English classical, the first instances of it in the building. Aymar Embury II also was responsible for the 1936 bronze stands at the Fifth Avenue and the 42nd Street entrances.

With the inevitable expansion of the Library, gallery space, once reserved for exhibitions, was taken over by administrative offices and special services. To be sure, an annex had been obtained in 1933, to be replaced by the present, larger one in 1961. After Lincoln Center was built, the Music, Dance and Theatre Collections and Divisions were moved in 1965 to a building of their own, the Performing Arts Research Center at Lincoln Center. The purchase of the old Arnold Constable Store, on the southeast corner of Fifth Avenue and 40th Street, for the Mid-Manhattan Branch in 1970 provided space for expansion and also relieved crowded conditions. The Circulation Branch, up to then housed in the main Library, the Children's Division, and other facilities and offices moved to the new building.

A similar effort occurred in the Periodical Division. Its two rooms, where DeWitt and Lila Acheson Wallace had worked when starting *The Reader's Digest,* were restored in 1983 and given murals by the DeWitt Wallace Foundation, and renamed the DeWitt Wallace Periodical Room.

The rehabilitation and improvements continue. For the reader, the most important has been the conversion of the Catalog Room, part of Room 315. Here, card trays have been replaced by bound volumes with book titles and authors. Computer terminals have been installed to speed book delivery. Room 316, formerly devoted to Photographic Services, once again became an exhibition gallery, the Edna B. Salomon Room.*

The restoration of these areas, begun in 1981, has accelerated under Dr. Vartan Gregorian, who became Library President in 1982. Pressure for more space, due to the incredible flow of printed matter, has prompted the changes. No less important has been the awakened interest in the Library's formidable collections and, of course, there is the building itself. All of these forces, along with an appreciative public, have spurred what is taking place now at this wonderful institution.

As we have seen, Thomas Hastings knew some disappointments at the Library, as did John Merven Carrère, but they are hardly the first great architects to suffer the occasional reverse. What is so extraordinary about the New York Public Library is how successful its building has been over the years and how successful it is still. John Shaw Billings posed a major challenge for John Merven Carrère and Thomas Hastings, to build an edifice at once useful and grand, and what is more, an edifice paid for by the people of New York. This challenge they met triumphantly by producing this people's palace, this great jewel of the civic crown of the City of New York.

*Individuals in charge of the restoration: Theodore S. Kinnari, preservationist, Manager of Capital Planning and construction for the Library; Theo Purdom, The Ehrenkrantz Group; Giorgio Cavaglieri, architect; Lewis Davis, architect, Davis Brody Associates; Arthur Rosenblatt, architect.

View of the Library at 41st Street and Fifth Avenue.

convex curve or belly dominating. Equally important in size and shape is their spacing, which has to be of such a width as to be pleasing to the eye. The ones here are eminently successful in every way.

An interesting comparison can be made between the baluster of Carrère & Hastings and the one of Jules Hardouin-Mansart, which is at the entrance to the Grand Trianon at Versailles.

Walking south or north, we come to beautiful bronze lampposts. New York has a variety of lampposts, the best of which were produced when the classical dominated civic design. There is the one on the ramp of the Grand Central Terminal by Warren & Wetmore; there is the old bishops's crook lamppost, the work of R. R. Bowker, founder of *Publisher's Weekly;* those in front of the American Museum of Natural History; the wrought iron ones in front of City Hall; and the ones by McKim, Mead & White on the Columbia University campus. These at the Library rank among the best. Once again we are reminded of the attention to detail on the part of Carrère & Hastings, a fact that will be evident again and again as we pursue our exploration of the Library.

The supreme ornament of the terrace is a pair of flagpole bases, one on the south and the other on the north. A plaque in the ground beside the northern one reads, "To Commemorate John Purroy Mitchel Mayor 1913–1914," and bears the city seal. The other, at the south base, reads, "In Honor of Major John Purroy Mitchel Died in Service 1918," and has the Great Seal of the United States. The pair was designed by Thomas Hastings and executed in the atelier of Lorenzo Rosario by the modellers Raffaele and Francesco Menconi with the figures being by a Mr. Grandelli. They were cast in the Tiffany Studios in 1912.

They are the most beautiful flagpole bases in the country and can be compared with any in the world, even with the handsome pair in Saint Mark's Square in Venice, possibly the first of their kind. We mentioned the role of the human figure in Western art. There is no better example of it to be seen than here. The four winged figures represent Navigation, holding a boat, Discovery holding a globe, Conquest drawing a sword, and Civilization holding a book.

A closer look at Navigation's boat will disclose the word *Argo* incised on its side. *Argo* was the name of the ship on which the legendary Greek hero Jason sailed with the Argonauts to steal the Golden Fleece.

The bases are encyclopedias of classical ornament. The essential form of the composition stems from a high-relief motif of a pagan altar, where a sacrificial beast was slaughtered. From this comes the adaptation of bucranes or skulls and garlands which adorned the beast

The bronze lamppost of the Library Terrace.

Conquest, *one of the four figures on a flag-pole base.*

The upper part of a flagpole base. The top of the double volutes resembles an owl's head. Between the volutes are three signs of the Zodiac: Scorpio, Sagittarius, and Capricorn.

A turtle at a flagpole base.

Oriental mask and cornucopias on a side of a flagpole base.

OPPOSITE. *One of the two flagpole bases, on the Library Terrace, designed by Thomas Hastings. The sculptors were Lorenzo Rosario, Raffaele and Francesco Menconi, and a Mr. Grandelli.*

being led to the sacrifice. Double volutes, linking the upper and lower parts of the base, have the shapes of sea horses. Pairs of cornucopias in relief are on the sides, between the figures. At the bottom are turtles, which carry the whole base. The style is High Renaissance, a Cellini candlestick enlarged.

Hastings' drawing for the base shows that changes occurred in the course of the modeling. A mask is added in the panel between the figures and, instead of resting on rams' heads, the base rests on turtles.

The flagpole, topped by an eagle, is eighty-seven feet high. The steps beneath the bronze are made of Tennessee/Knoxville marble.

A glance at a nearby bench shows that the design of it, too, was planned. Its pedestals show a recessed panel bordered by two volutes.

At the north and the south ends of the terrace are two small secondary terraces parallel to 40th Street and 42nd Street. At the steps leading to them are massive posts that have, on one side, the caduceus of the god Mercury set on a scroll frame. There is no symbolism here, just decoration, although, with today's interest in communication, Mercury's staff with its entwined snakes could well be revived as its symbol.

At the west end of these secondary terraces is a granite bench similar to the one near the lions. Instead of wreaths at the back, there is a band consisting of a Vitruvian scroll with acanthus in the interstices. On either side of the bench are posts with sunken panels; the panels are framed by a series of moldings.

The caduceus ornament, at the south and north ends of the Library Terrace.

At the northern secondary terrace the bench post has, on its western side, a large double volute serving as buttress. The size alone is impressive, but what makes it exemplary is the big curving acanthus leaf on its front. Just by itself it underscores the endless possibilities inherent in classical ornament.

Nearby, on the Library wall, are the Roman numerals MDCCCCII (1902) incised in a large block, the cornerstone, which was laid on November 10 of that year. On a sunny afternoon one thousand guests assembled to witness the ceremony. Dr. W. R. Huntington of Grace Church offered the invocation, the Honorable John Bigelow, president of the Library, made the address, Mayor Seth Low laid the stone, and Archbishop John Farley gave the benediction. The cornerstone contains the usual documents that seem customary for such safekeeping: annual reports, by-laws, rules, photographs of the city, newspapers of the day, and other items.

Unknown to the public, an unofficial cornerstone-laying had taken place earlier, on August 12. "Yesterday," wrote Dr. John Shaw Billings, the Library's first director, to his wife, "Carrère, Hastings and myself had a little private corner-stone laying, setting the first block of marble on the new building on the northwest corner. [That is, directly west of this point.] I took the trowel, spread the bed of mortar a little, Hastings dropped a new ten-cent piece (1902) into it, down came the stone, I tapped it three times with a hammer and said— 'May this building be all that the builders, the architects, the trustees, and the people of New York hope and expect.'" His wish was triumphantly fulfilled.

A large double volute with acanthus on the north secondary level of the Library Terrace.

The drawing by Thomas Hastings for a flagpole base on the Library Terrace.

The portico of the main entrance.

III

THE FACADE

WE HAVE HELD OFF from examining the building up to this point. The corner with the cornerstone is the most convenient spot to examine the structure's mighty base. The massiveness is conveyed by the size of the stones and the use of rustication, with the stone giving beveled edging. Below the rustication is a water table, as it is known, with the cyma reversa shape. Below it, in turn, is a high course of gray granite, not marble; the use of granite was standard in the base course of large classical buildings throughout the city. Above the rustication is a giant half-round called the torus.

The sense of strength, the massiveness that carries the facade is further conveyed by the batter or slight incline given the rusticated portion. Batter and rustication, the thick torus and the large cyma reversa may be visual, not structural, devices, but they are essential elements of the classical. In the classical tradition, it must be recalled, the visual is of equal importance as the structural and the functional.

There is no question about the massiveness of the building. The masonry of the walls consists of brick work four feet thick—there are no supporting steel posts. The Danby/Dorset marble from near Manchester, Vermont, which forms the revetment, averages a foot in thickness. The four-foot brick wall descends to a basement wall seven feet thick and, at the bottom, it spreads to between 13½ feet and 16 feet.

(A contrast in the depth of revetment is offered by the example of the Frick Collection at Fifth Avenue and 70th Street, also by Carrère & Hastings. There the courses of Indiana limestone are alternatively 8 and 4 inches thick.)

From the corner we go to the center of the terrace. The portico sets the tone of the whole. Rising from a flight of twenty steps are three arched bays framed by columns with high narrow walls on either side. What the architects did, in short, was to create an imperial entrance to the people's palace.

The eye is drawn to the attic, with its statues, from left to right, of History, Drama, Poetry, Religion, Romance, and Philosophy. They are the work of Paul Wayland Bartlett, who did the sculpture in the pediment of the House Wing of the United States Capitol. Bartlett was given $20,000 for the modeling, which was done in Paris because he, like a number of American artists, had a studio there. The actual carving was executed by Piccirilli Brothers for $5,000 in their Bronx studio.

It should be mentioned that the statues are eleven feet high. Such height is essential for figures placed so high and so distant from the observer. Were they any shorter they would appear grotesquely small.

Between the statues are three inscriptions left to right:

THE ASTOR LIBRARY
FOUNDED BY
JOHN JACOB ASTOR
(south) FOR THE
ADVANCEMENT OF USEFUL KNOWLEDGE
MDCCCXLVIII

THE LENOX LIBRARY
FOUNDED BY
JAMES LENOX
(center) DEDICATED TO HISTORY
LITERATURE AND THE FINE ARTS
MDCCCLXX

THE TILDEN TRUST
FOUNDED BY
SAMUEL JONES TILDEN
(north) TO SERVE THE INTERESTS OF
SCIENCE AND POPULAR EDUCATION
MDCCCLXXXVI

On the frieze is inscribed "MDCCCXCV THE NEW YORK PUBLIC LIBRARY MDCCCCXI," the year of the Library's founding and the year of the building's completion.

From the frieze the viewer's eye descends to the keystones of the

PAUL WAYLAND BARTLETT, 1865–1925, was born in New Haven, Connecticut, and went to Paris to study under Frémiet and Cavelier. He did animal groups that are in the Jardin des Plantes in Paris, the pediment of the House Wing of the United States Capitol, and assisted J. Q. A. Ward with the sculpture of the pediment of the New York Stock Exchange. He did the equestrian statues of General Washington in Philadelphia, of General Warren in Boston, and of General McClellan in Washington. His best-known statue is the equestrian of Lafayette which stood, until 1984, in front of the Louvre in Paris.

three arches. They bear three heads, of Juno, Minerva, and Mercury. Originally, the three, modeled by Philip Martiny, were all of Minerva, which the architects found unsatisfactory. Therefore, in 1909 the sculptor François Tonetti-Dozzi was commissioned to transform two of them into the heads of Juno and Mercury.

It is this pride that is evoked in stone all about us here. No better instrument of style for this exists than that of the classical tradition. It has the devices that other architectural styles simply do not have. For example, one of the ways the building strikes the viewer is by the height of the arched bays. But they would be bland if they were not placed atop a flight of steps and, of even greater importance, if they were without an abundance of ornament, as on the flagpole bases. The ornament here consists of Corinthian columns, set on pedestals adorned with Greek keys and rosettes.

As if all of this were insufficient, Carrère and Hastings placed two large vases of Tennessee Pink marble on the steps in front of the porch, no doubt inspired by the famous vases on the main terrace of the Palace of Versailles. They are 9 feet 8 inches high.

(Such vases, although not the architects' "signature," are to be found in front of the Fifth Avenue facade of The Frick Collection on Fifth Avenue at 70th Street. Carrère and Hastings designed that beautiful residence while working on the Library.)

Carrère & Hastings originally wanted monoliths, that is, single blocks of stone, for the column shafts. They decided instead to have drums measuring, in the main, the same height of most of the courses of the wall. The horizontal stone jointing is, in this way, not interrupted. The width of the shaft at its base is 3 feet 6 inches, the column height is 35 feet 4 inches. (By way of comparison, the height of the Corinthian column at the Metropolitan Museum of Art is 44 feet 4 inches.) Thus the ratio of ten diameters to one, Vignola's rule for the Corinthian order, has been followed, as shown by Orders of Architecture in the Glossary. It must be remembered that these column ratios—we will see how they apply to columns inside the building—are the result of a centuries-old tradition that aimed for beauty. For this reason, the study of the orders, Tuscan, Doric, Ionic, Corinthian, and Composite, is basic in classical instruction. There is probably no other way to acquire the skill not only to execute ornament, but also to achieve the right proportion and scale.

Mention of proportion and scale brings up a subject that is at the heart of the beautiful in architecture. Proportion is simply the relation of one part to another. With respect to the the column, it is the relation of the diameter of the shaft to column height, and of the part to the whole, here, the facade.

PHILIP MARTINY, sculptor, 1858–1927, was born in Strasbourg, France, where he studied under Eugène Dock. On coming to New York he worked for Augustus Saint-Gaudens, assisting him with the mantelpiece formerly in the Cornelius Vanderbilt mansion and now in the Metropolitan Museum of Art. He did the groups at the Hall of Records in New York and the spandrel figures on the Soldiers and Sailors Monument in Brooklyn. He was also responsible for the lions in front of the Boston Public Library and the cherubs of the grand staircase of the Library of Congress.

FRANÇOIS M. L. TONETTI-DOZZI, see chimney breast and mantelpiece in the Trustees' Room, p. 177.

Capitals, entablature and the head of Minerva by Philip Martiny.

Tragic and comic masks on the underside of the lip of the vase.

One of the two vases on the Library steps.

The architects' drawing for the vase on the Library steps. Note the differences with the final version, such as the greater variety in the masks.

The pedestal of the Library vase resting on lion paws. The relief consists of palmettes and husks joined by strap work.

The ancestor of both the Library and the Versailles vases. Reproduced from Volume 11 and 12 of Giovanni Battista Piranesi's *Opere*. Courtesy of the Cooper-Hewitt Museum, The Smithsonian Institution's National Museum of Design.

The Vase of Peace on the terrace of the Palace of Versailles. Photo Henry Hope Reed II.

Standing below the column, we know ourselves to be in human scale whereas the column is monumental in scale, as is the neighboring vase. That is as it should be because the large, well-proportioned, column conveys the importance of the building. The human figure is not the only contrast at this spot; the doorway inside the portico also serves the purpose. These doorways are somewhat larger than customary, as befits the building's size and importance, but not too large to reduce visually the nearby column.

The ratios of the shaft diameter and column height vary in a small way, depending on the materials used, where the columns stand, and their relation to the whole composition, in this case, the facade, but they are never far from the norm, otherwise they would be ugly.

By way of contrast, there is a very high single Corinthian column. It is part of the Bronx War Memorial on Shore Road in Pelham Bay Park, and stands seventy-five feet high on an eighteen-foot base. If this were part of a building, it would be way out of proportion, but as a single artifact standing alone it is successful, not the least because it carries a sixteen-foot figure of Victory.

It may seem strange to recall that it was the Ionic order, not the Corinthian order, that was in the winning design of the facade. The Corinthian is so much more effective that one wonders why the architects did not adopt it in the first place. The change represents a shift in accent from the horizontal to the vertical and also brings enrichment to the facade. The same shift was underscored in the wings, where fluted engaged Corinthian columns replaced flat Ionic pilasters.

One more factor makes the columns so wonderfully effective: the shafts, 33 feet 6 inches high, are not straight. While the base diameter, 3 feet 10½ inches, remains the same for the first third, the shaft then tapers, curving very gently to the top, where it is 3 feet 4 inches in diameter. This shaping of the profile is called entasis, a device perfected by the ancient Greeks. Were the profile of the shaft straight, it would appear to have convex sides; the slight tapering corrects the optical illusion, for if the column does not appear straight, it has a pleasing silhouette.

Carrère and Hastings had their feet well planted in the classical, always drawing on its wealth. The classical artist has never claimed to have invented the artistic wheel. The Library's Corinthian capital is an example. The building's archive mentions that the architects took as guide the capital of one of Gabriel's famous buildings in the Place de la Concorde in Paris. They obtained a plaster model of it, in all probability from the Ecole des Beaux Arts, which possessed a collection of molds of decorative elements of great buildings. They

A Corinthian capital of the Fifth Avenue facade.

The architects' drawing for the Corinthian capital. It is reproduced here because its detail is easier to "read" than that of the photograph. Courtesy Building Maintenance and Operations Department, New York Public Library, Astor, Lenox and Tilden Foundations.

could have as easily turned to Roman examples such as the Temple of Concord, the Temple of Castor and Pollux, and the Pantheon (see *Fragments from Greek and Roman Architecture,* The Classical America Edition Hector d'Espouy's Plates in this Series). They could not copy it due to the fact that they were working with an entirely different stone, a white Vermont marble instead of a French limestone of gray cream, because of the different light of New York and the massiveness of their building compared to Gabriel's.

We offer illustrations of the two capitals. While parts match, as they do on any number of Corinthian capitals, there are key differences, notably in the spaces between the leaves and the shape of the leaves themselves. For example, the Library acanthus has large lobes and small clefts, that of the Paris building has just the opposite.

Again, we have to remind ourselves that in the classical tradition there is the ever-present turning to the past, and that, in doing so, the classical eye is always seeking out ornament. It is an essential ingredient in obtaining the best proportion and scale.

The wings carry the main motif of the porch. The bays are divided by the same Corinthian columns, but they are engaged instead of being freestanding. They stand on the rusticated base that we examined earlier. In the bays are tall, round-arched windows with balustrades. On the arches are keystones with lion heads holding rings; they might have been taken from Venetian moorings but are actually based on a model by Alexander Phimister Proctor, specialist in animal sculpture. The heads link the arch keystone to the framing of the windows of the second floor.

We have discussed the purpose of adopting a colossal order and the use of contrast as in the of the doorways and of the human form. On the wings, the size of the columns is emphasized by the fact that they embrace two stories. Their apparent height is thus increased.

At the ends of the wings are shallow extensions where the bays, still with single columns, are framed by walls much as is the central portico. But instead of an attic they have pediments, triangular spaces above the entablature. They are filled with sculpture, the work of George Grey Barnard, whose collection of medieval architectural fragments was purchased by John D. Rockefeller, Jr., to form the kernel of the Cloisters in Fort Tryon Park, at the north end of Manhattan.

In the south pediment, two figures, male and female, recline on either side of a globe. The man holds a chisel in his right hand and a hammer in his left. The woman has two large books on her right knee. They represent The Arts. History is the subject of the north pediment. A female figure is inscribing the word *Life* in an open book.

A Corinthian capital from the Ministry of the Marine on the Place de la Concorde in Paris.

A lion mask with ring, part of the keystone of the first floor windows modeled by Alexander Phimister Proctor.

The Arts by George Grey Barnard in the south pediment of the Fifth Avenue facade.

History by George Grey Barnard in the north pediment of the Fifth Avenue facade.

In walking back and forth, one may well wonder why there is a balustrade above the cornice between the central attic and the end pediments. After all, a balustrade is presumably used to serve as a guard and a device to lean on. It has a double purpose: in this instance, to conceal a roof and, more important, to give scale. This balustrade is 4 feet 10 inches high, somewhat higher than customary; the ones we lean on range from three to four feet in height, as at the terrace. But because it is on the roof, a certain liberty is permitted and, in addition, it is set on a high plinth course. (On big buildings, such St. Peter's Basilica in Rome, balustrades assume colossal heights; there they stand about eight feet high.)

To either side of the portico are fountains, perhaps the best in the city. They are set in bays bordered by vertical rustication rising to the main entablature. Note how the rustic work, the channeling between the stones, alternates at each course. With one it is wholly flat, with the other there is a raised panel. Each fountain fronts on a niche that has, at the top, the now familiar lion head on its volute with imbricated leaves and with oak leaf sprays to either side.

The fountains are magnificent; each consists of a series of basins wonderfully adorned. The water pours from the mouth of a satyr mask in full relief. Just as the couchant lions form the first evidence of the beast in the Library's decoration, so does this stone satyr announce the presence of this mythical figure. Satyrs in the Ancient World were wood spirits, half man and half goat. Lascivious, cowardly, and given to drink, they were symbolic of the luxuriant forces of nature and were frequently associated with Bacchus. They came to have a place in the vocabulary of classical ornament, particularly in the form of a mask. The satyr mask was one of the ancient ornaments discovered and adopted by the Italian Renaissance; by 1520 it was already in common use. Michelangelo's first piece of sculpture, now lost, is presumed to have been that of a satyr mask.

The cornucopia and the turtle make a second appearance on the fountains.

Above the south fountain, in the niche, is the figure of a young woman seated on a Pegasus, or winged horse. (Pegasus, sprung from the blood of Medusa when she was slain by Perseus, was a favorite of the Muses and, in modern times, has become symbolic of poetic inspiration.) The young woman represents Beauty, as revealed in the inscription above the lion head: beauty old yet ever new eternal voice and inward word. The brief passage is from *The Shadow and Light* by the poet John Greenleaf Whittier. On the north fountain a bearded, baldheaded man is seated on a sphinx; he stands for Truth. The

ALEXANDER PHIMISTER PROCTOR, sculptor, 1862-1950. He was born in Ontario, Canada, and raised in Denver, Colorado. He studied at the Arts Students League and the National Academy of Design in New York and, later in Paris. He did major work at the World's Columbian Exposition of 1893 in Chicago. He modeled horses for Augustus Saint-Gaudens, notably that of General Sherman on Fifth Avenue and 59th Street in New York. He also worked for Carrère & Hastings at the Pan-American Exposition of 1901 in Buffalo. Among his work are the two panthers at an entrance to Prospect Park in Brooklyn and animal sculpture in the Bronx Zoo. His best known statues are "The Pioneer Mother" and "The Bronco Buster."

GEORGE GREY BARNARD, sculptor, 1863–1917, was born in Bellefonte, Pennsylvania, the son of a Presbyterian minister. He studied at the Chicago Art Institute in 1880 and three years later was in the Paris atelier of Pierre-Jules Cavelier. In 1886 he found a patron in Alfred Corning Clark, of the family that, at one time, owned the Singer Sewing Machine Company. Barnard is best known for the figure of Pan on the Columbia University campus and the figure groups on the terrace of the Pennsylvania State Capitol in Harrisburg, as well as his connection with the Cloisters in Fort Tryon Park, New York.

The south fountain of the Library with the statue of Beauty by Frederick MacMonnies.

Volutes with acanthus and ribbon, panels of stalagtites, an enriched cornucopia with a lizard at the top, and a turtle beneath a scallop shell, on the south fountain.

inscription overhead is from the Book of Esdras, I:13, as found in the King James version of the Bible: "Above all things, Truth bear-

eth away the victory." Both statues are the work of Frederick MacMonnies, best known for the bronze groups on America's greatest triumphal arch, the Soldiers and Sailors Monument in Brooklyn.

The style of the sculpture is naturalistic, rather than classical. Obviously, MacMonnies modelled them on particular living individuals, rather than on a distillation of figures both live and antique.

The whole and the parts of the great facade are so joined that the composition is one of the city's wonders. There are the lion heads, the voluted keystones, the helmeted heads on the portico, the Corinthian capitals, all the panoply of the tradition. The handling of the columns, the manner in which the porch and pedimented pavilions at the end of the wings are framed, the distribution of ornament— together they indicate that this is a triumph of classical architecture produced by men who had gone to the Ecole des Beaux Arts. Certain commentators have criticized the presence of so much ornament, the imbricated volutes, the lion masks with their rings, and the sculpture. But classical architecture, observed John Barrington Bayley in his *Letarouilly on Renaissance Rome* (in this Series), is like the sea. One moment it lies calm, as in the Greek Revival with its serene colonnades; at another it is storm-tossed with dramatic play of chiaroscuro, as in the Baroque. If, for some, there are shortcomings here, the magisterial view may well be to hold that this facade is to be enjoyed as one more aspect of the classical sea, which, at its best, is always different and never repeats.

Satyr mask, cornucopias, scallop shells, and turtles on the south fountain.

FREDERICK MACMONNIES, sculptor, 1863–1937, was born in Brooklyn and began his career at sixteen in the studio of Augustus Saint-Gaudens. A stint in Paris followed in the Atelier Falguière. He came to prominence on executing the "Ship of State," a boat with many figures in the Court of Honor at the World's Columbian Exposition of 1893. He did the spandrel figures in the Washington Arch in Washington Square and the Nathan Hall statue in City Hall Park, both in New York. Other the Soldiers and Sailors Monument he did the statue of J. S. T. Stranahan and the Horse Tamers in Prospect Park, in Brooklyn. He did the winged Victory for the Battle Monument at West Point, the Pioneer Monument in Denver, the equestrian General McClellan and the bronze entrances of the Library of Congress both in Washington, and the Princeton Battle Monument in Princeton, New Jersey.

IV

THE PORTICO

THE OPULENCE OF THE PORTICO is hardly to be accepted as merely an element of the facade. The portico has often been called an exterior vestibule. There is a special pleasure in the soft light caressing the white marble, especially on a bright sunny day. There is something familiar about the combination of the marble and the soft light, which is seen at the Lincoln Memorial in Washington or the Propylaea on the Acropolis, the triumphal gateway to the Parthenon. In any weather, there is a calm to be enjoyed just by standing here, if only as contrast to the changing throng on the avenue below. Few things can equal the portico in its contribution to the monumentality of a building, as it does so beautifully here.

The portico consists of three divisions crowned by barrel vaults. Separating each, somewhat lower, are two wide arches at right angles. The soffits of the latter are decorated with rosette-filled coffers set in a diamond pattern. The soffits of the barrel vaults are more restrained, having two bands of beribboned grape vines and bunches of grapes rising from vases in relief. The vaults rise from a cornice with the familiar lion head on a double volute, imbricated on the front and with oak leaf sprays on the sides.

A particularly handsome feature of the porch are the two niches at either end. Again, the diamond-coffering is repeated, this time in the semidomes.

The constant repetition of ornamental detail is one of the rewards

The soffit of the portico arch with its diamond grid and rosettes.

OPPOSITE. *The portico interior.*

of classical architecture. This is true even of the lion masks. Only when human masks are too often repeated does the decoration grow dull; there has to be some variety when the human face or figure is involved.

Standing in the north niche and looking south, one has a perspective of the noble devices that make the portico so splendid: the high arches to either side, the exterior column on the left and the pedimented doorway on the right, the arches and the vaults, and, at the opposite end, the twin niche serving as focus.

[Three large bronze globes, four feet in diameter, were recently placed in the three bays. They were modeled on the globes to be found in the South-North Gallery of the first floor.]

On the west side of the porch the bays are partly open. The upper halves are glazed, whereas the lower halves are filled with marble doorways. Each consists of a pediment resting on a modified entablature. To either side, just below the frieze, is open strapwork, in the middle of which are L's placed thus ⅃L, framed by a bayleaf wreath.

The arch and beyond, the semidome of the niche.

ASTOR HALL

OPPOSITE. *A candelabrum in Astor Hall.*

WHAT WE HAVE EXPLORED, in the portico, is part of a foreshortened triumphal way. It began on Fifth Avenue and, at every step, we were presented with devices to make the way more splendid, with the visual climax within the building—Astor Hall. And we find ourselves not only in the climax of one triumphal way but at the start of another, which will end at the Main reading Room.

Astor Hall is a rectangular room 76 feet 6 inches long and 47 feet deep, with a vault 37 feet 3½ inches overhead. The room is framed by ten piers, which divide the sides into ten round-arch bays. The bays on the long sides to the east and west have the piers framed by Doric columns. Column and pier are topped by an entablature with a deep cornice, which serves as an impost for the arches and the vault above. The entablature and the bays in balance underline the visual unity here—unity being an element so essential in any art, let alone architecture. This unity with balance and symmetry induces calm and, while inducing calm, makes the visitor look about.

The entablature, actually a series of entablatures repeated around the room, is of interest in itself. Here we cannot help remarking on several particular imprints of the architects. We expect the guttae, the six drops beneath the cornice, also found on the soffit of the mutule above eighteen here, although there are customarily thirty-six as we know from *The American Vignola* (in this Series) and we are surprised to discover the relief of a bee at the corner. The architects modified the entablature by omitting the frieze, there being only cornice and architrave. Even the architrave changes: on the east and west sides of the room, it is made up of two fascias, whereas each of the two three other sides has only one. These are only some of the variations found in a great classical buildings.

What is extraordinary is the way the bays serve different functions, yet the unity is in no way impaired. For example, the bays of the east side are part of the portico bays and contain the pedimented doorways. Those opposite, on the west side, are open to permit access to a corridor running south and north. The columns, 17 feet 6½ inches high on a pedestal 1 foot 6¾ inches high, serve to accent these two long sides. By way of contrast to the columns, the bay arches rise 32 feet.

At the base, the column shaft has a diameter of 2 feet 3 inches, at the top, 2 feet. The shafts are monolithic, in contrast to those outside, which are made of drums. (Monolithic columns were known to the Egyptians and the Romans, but not to the Greeks.)

The marble vault has a special fascination because it consists of voussoirs, or wedge-shaped blocks, so fitted as to be self-supporting. Stone rooms of this size are rare. Astor Hall must be one of the few rooms in the world made entirely of marble. In Paris there is a large stone room in the Palace of Justice but it is of limestone. Such stone work, known as stereotomy or the art of shaping stones, was very much part of French architecture.

While this stereotomic vault is designed to be self-sustaining, it is, in truth, affixed to the floor above by a layer of concrete. The architects wanted to avoid spalling, that is, chipping or flaking at the edges, which might have occurred had the stones alone supported the pressure.

Entrance halls are of stone because they are still, in part, exterior rooms. The rule in classical building is a progression. Materials become more delicate as one leaves the entrance, stone giving place to wood, painted plaster, tapestry, and, eventually, damask. In the Library, stone and imitation stone are more conspicuous because of French influence. (Among other New York buildings in which this influence is equally conspicuous are the National Academy of Design at 1083 Fifth Avenue, formerly the residence of Archer M. Huntington, designed by Ogden Codman, Jr.; the James Buchanan Duke mansion at 1 East 78th Street, now New York University's Institute of Fine Arts, by Horace Trumbauer and the Frick Collection at 2 East 70th Street, which was designed by Carrère & Hastings, with additions by John Russell Pope and John Barrington Bayley.)

Doric columns in Astor Hall.

The entablature and capital in Astor Hall. A bee is seen on the soffit or underside of the cornice.

OPPOSITE. *Astor Hall from south to north.*

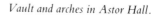
Vault and arches in Astor Hall.

Detail of the vault of Astor Hall.

The bay arches result in transverse vaults that penetrate the main segmental vault. The penetrations, however, leave a large surface, which is broken into rectangles framed by richly ornamented borders.

The two piers directly opposite the entrance bear the following inscriptions, the first on the left, the second, on the right.

THE CITY OF NEW YORK
HAS ERECTED THIS BUILDING
TO BE MAINTAINED AS A FREE LIBRARY
FOR THE USE OF THE PEOPLE
ON THE DIFFUSION OF EDUCATION
AMONG THE PEOPLE
REST THE PRESERVATION
AND PERPETUATION
OF OUR FREE INSTITUTIONS

In recent decades, the wide piers have been adopted as pylons to honor donors to the Library, whose names are incised on the marble surface. The list of these names is to be found in Appendix III.

The pattern of the floor which is divided into squares and circles, repeats the pattern of the portico floor. It made of the same kind of marble, gray Siena and Hauteville, and is 1⅜ inches thick. The walls, the monoliths and the vaulting are of Danby/Dorset.

In the center of the floor is an inscription:

INSCRIBED HERE ARE THE WORDS OF AN
IMMIGRANT WHOSE LIFE WAS TRANSFORMED BY THE
LIBRARY AND WHOSE ESTATE NOW ENRICHES IT.
IN MEMORY
MARTIN RADTKE
1883–1973
I HAD LITTLE OPPORTUNITY FOR FORMAL EDUCATION
AS A YOUNG MAN IN LITHUANIA, AND I AM DEEPLY
INDEBTED TO THE NEW YORK PUBLIC LIBRARY
FOR THE OPPORTUNITY TO EDUCATE MYSELF.
IN APPRECIATION, I HAVE GIVEN THE LIBRARY
MY ESTATE WITH THE WISH THAT IT BE USED SO
THAT OTHERS CAN HAVE THE SAME OPPORTUNITY
MADE AVAILABLE TO ME.

A bold addition to the hall are two pairs of marble candelabra or lamp standards that contribute assumptuous note. They are of Roman inspiration; their models are to be found in the Gallery of the Vases and Candelabra in the Pio Clementino Museum of the Vatican. It is worth noting Thomas Hastings' comment on their design: "Still another form of architectural ornament is the candelabrum. The problem to be solved in this case was to make a stanchion of considerable length which would stand on end. A superposition of different forms in this length was therefore necessary. The truncated form of the pedestal lifted on feet, sometimes on a tripod, is a very common way of beginning such a superposition. The spreading lines giving the candelabrum support. On this pedestal stands a second general division in the form of a baluster with an Ionic cap [here it is Doric], supporting the third or final division in the form of a saucer. On these general structural forms as foundations the artist may give his imagination free scope to decorate and to enrich." Certainly Carrère and Hastings did not hesitate to accept that challenge. Garlanded and beribboned bucranes appear again, and so do ox hooves, mentioned in this study for the first time. Among the acanthus leaves and rosettes of the shaft are dolphins, and the bronze arms of the lamps have the familiar lion head. The marble is Carrara from Carrara in the Apennine Alps, Italy.

There is one all-marble setting in the porch. Here is another, at once more subdued and more spacious, with its play of penetrations. Within the monochromatic setting, so sumptuous as a result of marble being on all sides, the architects introduced a soothingly contrasting notes in the ornament of the vault, in the Doric columns, and not least in the candelabra, where their skill produced a rare beauty.

The base of the candelabrum, consisting of ox hooves, bucranes with garlands and ribbons, and acanthus leaves.

A candelabrum in Astor Hall.

The candelabrum shaft with dolphins, rosettes, and acanthus.

The top of the candelabrum. Godroons shape the bottom of the saucer, from which rises a scotia embellished with acanthus. The bronze arms are all acanthus with lion heads.

The profile of a bronze arm of the candelabrum, with its lion head.

The bronze door of the Gottesman Exhibition Hall.

THE GOTTESMAN EXHIBITION HALL (Room 113)

WE WALK THROUGH a central arched opening in the long South-North Gallery. A portion of this gallery, next to Astor Hall, consists of five bays separated by four, wide, transverse arches, with narrow transverse arches at either end. Overhead, in each bay, is a flat ceiling with elaborate dark brown and gold decoration in low relief. In the classical canon, flat ceilings, such as these, have to be broken up into sunken panels, or coffering, and enriched with detail. This detail is not always easy to make out, but that is one of the rewards of the classical. Not every aspect of it is perceived at first glance, any more than a passage in a symphony or an opera registers on first hearing. No doubt it will come as a surprise that there are two satyr masks overhead. Or that there are small panels made of modified scallop shells centered on rosettes.

The five-bay section of the South-North Gallery is repeated to the west in a short corridor or foyer. This foyer is bound to the Gallery by a repetition of decorative treatment. The five round-arched bays are paralleled by a west wall that is varied in the following manner: at either end of the wall are square-arched windows with keystone and sides of curved chamfering. Between them are three round-arched bays, which are duplicates, the central one with a doorway leading to the Gottesman Exhibition Hall and two blind ones to either side. Inside these three bays are pedimented doorways whose frames are the mates of those of the east wall of Astor Hall. Similarly, two bays, both round-arched and both with pedimented doorways, are at the

The view north along the South-North Gallery. The bust of Julius Caesar is in the niche in the center of the photograph.

The rosette on the soffit or underside of the arch between Astor Hall and the South-North Gallery.

Satyr mask on the flat central ceiling of the South-North Gallery.

On the flat ceiling of the South-North Gallery, a sunken panel framed with a cyma reversa embellished with acanthus carries a rosette surrounded by four modified scallop shells.

A view of the southwest bay of Astor Hall leading to the foyer beyond the South-North Gallery. This is an example of the play of space in the Library.

south and north ends of the foyer. The south one is for the Frederick Lewis Allen Room, Room 112, named for the well-known editor of *Harper's Magazine* and the north one is for the Library Shop, Room 116. A distinction of the doorways is the frieze with the foliated chain band with rosettes, also to be seen, on the right, in the reveal of the sides and the square arch of the window.

The doorway to the Frederick Lewis Allen Room. The frieze beneath the pediment has a foliated chain band with rosettes, as does the reveal of the window on the right.

To provide even greater freedom of movement for visitors to the Library, to bring visual balance, and to obtain additional penetrations in perspective, the four massive piers between the Gallery and the foyer have square-arched openings. Their size and shape reflect those of the niches on the east side of the Gallery. These niches are repeated on the foyer's west wall. Decorating the blind niches, that is, those filled with a wall, are splendid brackets with the busts of Titus, Sophocles, Terence, Julius Caesar, Brutus, Demosthenes, and Pompey by Leone Clerici The great men of the Ancient World could not be more fittingly mounted. Again and again, Carrère and Hastings, by continuous use of repetition and balance, strove for visual unity, which is so important in achieving beauty.

To either side of the southernmost square-arched niche of the west foyer wall are plaques listing the names of those of the Library staff who served in World War I and World War II. They are to be found in Appendix IV.

The D. Samuel and Jeane H. Gottesman Exhibition Hall was restored in 1984 through the gifts of many donors, of whom the D. S. and R. H. Gottesman Foundation gave $1,250,000. Supplementing this were the $1,000,000 contribution of the Rockefeller Brothers Fund, Inc.; $300,000 from the Uris Brothers Foundation, Inc.; and $150,000 from Harold W. McGraw, Jr., a Library trustee. Other donors were Dr. Margaret Brown, Mrs. Robert D. Graff, Mrs. Iola Haverstick, Mrs. August G. Paine, Mr. and Mrs. Peter Paine, and Mrs. Carleton Palmer.

The door to the Gottesman Exhibition Hall has the vitality and the freshness inherent in great metal work. Inevitably, we seek comparisons elsewhere in the nation and abroad. The wrought iron doors of Marble House in Newport, Rhode Island, or those of the Duke mansion of Fifth Avenue and 78th Street in New York City come to mind. The stair railings in the United States Capitol and the San Francisco City Hall offer equally intricate detail. The inspiration for Carrère and Hastings, and for most of the metal doors of this kind, is the wrought iron door for the Château de Maisons (ca. 1650), designed by the architect François Mansart; it now guards the entrance to the Gallery of Apollo in the Louvre, in Paris.

The design of the door in the Library, starting with a rectangular frame of guilloche filled with imbricated disks, has a field of openwork rinceaux. On each panel there is an oval frame of reeds partially wrapped by acanthus. A second frame follows, consisting of two semicircles, each ending in rosette volutes that are joined by hyphenbearing disks. The half circles are channeled with the channels filled with acanthus-shaped bells. And, finally, on the inside is a shield bearing the letters PL. A pair of snakes is to be seen to either side of the shield with their heads protruding through it. At the top of it all is a spread-wing eagle.

The lever handle of the door is one of several that are found in the Library. This called is the "torch handle" because of the torch bor-

The bust of Julius Caesar on a monumental bracket.

The central panel of the bronze door of the Exhibition Hall.

The eagle on the door to the Exhibition Hall.

The "torch" lever handle of the bronze door, with the torch bordered by a sprig of bay.

The wrought iron door from the Château de Maisons designed by François Mansart, at the entrance to the Gallery of Apollo in the Louvre. Photo Henry Hope Reed II.

dered by sprigs of bay. The end consists of a volute with an acanthus leaf, and the part attached to the bolt has a knob of modified acanthus ringed by half-sunken disks. The plate, as it is called, has a border of ribbon. All the door handles, door rings, and door plates were made by the Russell-Erwin Company of New Britain, Connecticut.

The posts to either side of the door were often treated as an order, in this case, a modified Corinthian, with acanthus leaves and volutes. There is even a fleuron made of an acanthus cup holding grapes. Equally fine is the bracket above, with its double volute enriched with acanthus and imbricated scales. It is a brilliant handing of ornament.

The marble frame of the doorway has a pediment resting on voluted ancones with acanthus. From the lower volute is suspended a rosette with a cluster of oak leaves and flowers. On the frieze between the ancones are circles, joined by double hyphens and filled with rosettes, called a foliated rosette band.

On the inside of the hall, the top of the doorway remains the same,

The Corinthian capital and bracket at the bronze door.

Inside the doorway of the Exhibition Hall.

but the frieze is different. Instead of the hyphenated circles is a rinceau in deep relief in whose center is a vase in relief from which billow puffs of smoke.

The Gottesman Exhibition Hall is 83 feet 3 inches long and 77 feet wide, with a ceiling 18 feet 10 inches high. On both sides of a central axis are two large piers wide enough to be pierced by an arch opening. On the center side of the piers are Ionic pilasters, while on the other sides are Ionic columns with monolithic shafts. The columns are repeated on the north and south sides of the hall; there are twenty-four in all. The marble here is Danby/Dorset from Vermont. Originally, the architects wanted a green Connemara marble from Ire-

The Exhibition Hall.

Pier arch and Ionic columns in the Exhibition Hall.

land. A favorite of the architect Charles Follen McKim, it is found in the entrance hall of the University Club, in the Low Library of Columbia University, and in the the Gould Library of the Bronx Community College. That marble was considered too costly, and a Cippolino marble was suggested instead. (A good example of Cippolino, from the Canton of Vaud, Switzerland, is to be seen in the lobby of the old United States Customs House on Bowling Green. The entrance hall of the Morgan Library has Cippolino columns.) This, too, was passed over. Finally, the architects had shafts made of Danby/Dorset marble so cut from the blocks with pronounced streaks that the graining was vertical instead of horizontal, as is found in the quarry bed. The piers and walls of the hall are from the same source, only the stone is laid with the graining horizontal. Such were the pains that the architects took to obtain here the contrasting effect of vertical and horizontal graining.

A detail of the arch and its attic. An oak branch with leaf-and-dart border is in the spandrel. The keystone with its stopped channeling, imbrication, acanthus, and volute is to be found in several locations in the building.

Each column is 1 foot 9½ inches in diameter at the base of the shaft, 1 foot 6½ inches at the top, and the shaft is 13 feet 9 inches high. Altogether, the column height, that is, base, shaft, and capital (but not including the pedestal) is 15 feet 9 inches.

Overhead is one of the most beautiful ceilings in the country. Certainly it is unusual in that it is of elaborately carved wood. It can only be measured against the ceiling of the Music Room, a double cube, of the William A. Clark, Jr., Library in Los Angeles, which, although of wood, was executed in a wholly different interpretation of the classical. The carver of the ceiling in the New York Public Library was Maurice Grieve.

Winged figures, cherubs, satyr masks, acanthus, fruit garlands, palmettes, and arabesques were part of Grieve's artistic vocabulary. A device that was introduced in the Renaissance and was therefore unknown to the ancients was the scroll frame. It almost always accompanies a cartouche or a shield and is customarily identified by volutes or scrolls. The frame looks as though it were made of cut boiled leather, and the edges are turned as if to show the thickness of the "leather." Thomas Hastings explained that this kind of cartouche with scroll frame was "frequently used as a motive for decoration where a place is to be enriched in the general composition of the building."

It is possible that John Barrington Bayley was the only authority to point out that the ceiling was the most neglected part of the American room. Commenting on the American failure in his *Letarouilly on Renaissance Rome* (in this Series), he wrote "the 'innocents abroad' look at ceilings, but the innocents at home ignore them." And he

An octagonal panel with winged figures, a winged cherub head, and a satyr mask on the ceiling of the Exhibition Hall.

explained that "a ceiling is the largest uninterrupted surface in any room, and presently the greatest of all opportunity for decoration." He primarily had residences and apartments in mind, but his observations apply with equal cogency to public buildings. The Library is something of an exception, because of the opulence and the variety of its ceilings, starting inside the portico and extending to the Trustees' Room.

In the center of the Exhibition Hall the piers serve to underscore the axis that begins at the main entrance of the building and continues through the hall to a glass door. Looking through it we can discern the main stacks. This is the only public glimpse of them. In the Library, books are not to be seen until we reach the reading rooms. Only here do we catch a glimpse of the ordered rows that make the New York Public Library a major resource to the city and to the nation. A winged cherub head appears in the bronze work.

A winged figure from the octagonal ceiling panel of the Exhibition Hall.

A winged figure on the ceiling of the Exhibition Hall.

A winged cherub blowing a trumpet on the ceiling of the Exhibition Hall.

ABOVE. A satyr mask on the ceiling of the Exhibition Hall.

LEFT. A satyr mask on the ceiling of the Exhibition Hall.

The mask of Diana on the ceiling of the Exhibition Hall.

A panel with four winged cherubs on the Exhibition Hall ceiling.

THE SOUTH-NORTH GALLERY. DEWITT WALLACE PERIODICAL ROOM (Room 108) MAP DIVISION (Room 117) SCIENCE AND TECHNOLOGY RESEARCH CENTER (Room 121)

WE RETURN TO the South-North Gallery, which we crossed on the way to the Exhibition Hall. The Gallery is 326 feet long, 14 feet 4 inches wide, and 20 feet 3 inches high. The floor is of the same gray Siena and dark-cream Hauteville and is one and three-eighths inches thick; the walls are finely rusticated Pentelic marble from Mount Pentelikon outside of Athens. This is the milky white marble of the Parthenon. It is pleasant to dwell on this association, one more link to our Mediterranean heritage. At the top of the rustication a modified cornice and frieze join wall and ceiling.

Of course, what invites the eye are the globes that light the gallery. Other than being a delight in themselves, the globes punctuate the length of the vista and make it apprehensible. They are, supremely, the servants of perspective.

The thirteen globes are made of thick pieces of curved glass with beveled edges. The glass is set in bronze frames decorated with cable molding. The skeleton was originally of a dark finish with the cable molding in gold, to form a contrast. Today, skeleton and molding are both gold, and the light they offer brighter than formerly.

The style of the Gallery is Franco-Roman but, again, as with Astor Hall, one would normally think of the great buildings of Europe to seek a comparison. However galleries in the Louvre and the Vatican, palaces, and châteaux are not relevant here. Nor, for that matter, is the central corridor that divides the ground floor of the great Bourbon palace at Caserta. The New York Public Library's Gallery stands by itself, a great hall of the highest mastery of severity and perspective.

Looking south, we can see how the rustication of the marble walls, and the modified cornice, underline the perspective. In contrast to the white Pentelic marble, the ceiling is gold on brown, softening the severity of the walls. Differing from the flat panels of the east-west axis, the ceiling is divided into a coffering of hexagons, octagons, and rectangles filled with rosettes. The coffers are separated by raised frames with soffits in guilloche.

At the south end of the gallery, a corridor opens on the right. It is guarded by a bronze grille-gate, which would appear to be inspired by the Spanish classical. The upper part of the door, with two grilles on either side, consists of an upright rectangle with spindles having candelabrum-like swellings of acanthus leaves, while the tops are much modified Corinthian capitals and the bottoms have been given a leaf treatment. Below, separated by a guilloche band and acanthus husks is another small rectangle, also of open work. Griffons melt into rinceaux with rosettes. Such grilles are known in Spain as *rejas*.

An octagonal coffer in the ceiling of the South-North Gallery.

The bronze grille-gate at the south end of the South-North Gallery.

The bottom of the grille at the south end of the South-North Gallery.

Opposite, on the left side of the gallery, is the entrance to the DeWitt Wallace Periodical Room, Room 108. The name of the room is indicated by the lettering in gilt italics incised in the marble to the left of the doorway. The doorway is in the purest Roman manner; it might be based on a doorway from Rome's Palazzo Mattei. The door is of oak simply treated. The ornament is confined to the lever handles that, on examination, prove to be the same as that of the door of the Gottesman Exhibition Hall, that is, the "torch handle."

On the inside, the drop rings have replaced the lever handles, but the visitor will find two new kinds of plates, escutcheon plates, one to each door leaf. The one on the left, from the inside out, has leaf-and-dart, pearl and leaf-and dart moldings. The other, on the right, has cross sprays of bay bound by fluttering ribbons and they are framed by two bands of scales; the whole is crowned by a cavetto of stopped fluting and a rosette knob in relief.

The DeWitt Wallace Periodical Room is so named because its restoration in 1983 was made possible by a gift of the DeWitt Wallace Foundation. Here, in this room, DeWitt Wallace and his wife, Lila Acheson Wallace, began their magazine *The Reader's Digest*. Here they read through magazines and copied articles for republication.

The room is 37 feet 2 inches by 44 feet with a 20-foot-4-inch-high ceiling. The same effortless symmetry and balance found in Astor Hall are found here. But instead of being divided by piers, round-arched bays are set in the wall. On the east and south sides, the bays frame windows; on the north side are a doorway and a delivery desk; and on the west there are a bay and a doorway.

The doorway illustrates the word opulent. Made of blue-gray Formosa marble from Wetzlar, Nassau, Germany, it is 10 feet 8 inches high, an impressive fact in itself, but it is the frieze and the pediment that provide the sumptuous accent. The marble is the only fossiliferous stone in the building identified by Stromatoporoids, resembling sponges.

Formosa marble runs around the base of the wall; it is also found at the doorway leading to a second room, part of Room 108, where the main delivery desk is to be found. In the floor, the perimeter is dark cream Hauteville with an inner band of Red Champlain "Oriental Variety" from Swanton, Vermont. The rest of the floor is covered with red quarry tile from Wales; this tile is found in all the rooms that are heavily used.

The eye quickly shifts to the extraordinary ceiling resting on an equally extraordinary cornice and frieze. What we see is a surface divided by deeply sunken panels in a variety of shapes and of orna-

An escutcheon plate and drop ring of the door of the DeWitt Wallace Periodical Room, Room 108.

OPPOSITE. *First of the two rooms that form part of the Periodical Room.*

The inside of a doorway of the Periodical Room.

ment in high relief, all of which is placed around a large central oval. The excuse for the particular treatment of the ceiling was the presence of two beams running east and west about four feet below the structural ceiling with the consequence that they came below the tops of the windows. It took Thomas Hastings a year to find the solution. If we were to go behind the plaster of the ceiling, for it is plaster stained to resemble wood, we would find the beams running parallel alongside the north and south sides of the oval. The presence of the beams helps to explain the six semidomes that penetrate the ceiling not only at the three windows, one facing east on Fifth Avenue and

The broken pediment of the entrance doorway of the Periodical Room with its scroll shield, with a lion mask, and two cornucopias.

two facing south on 40th Street, but also at the three bays opposite the windows.

The ceiling is quite overwhelming. For that reason it is easier to examine it in parts. The frame of the rectangle around the oval brings together a half-dozen kinds of enrichment. Much of it can be found in the picture (See Identifications) of the corner of the same rectangle which has the added embellishment of a large acanthus leaf. Even the cap of the socket from which a chandelier hangs has a circlet of egg-and-dart. An unusual piece of decoration is the cartouche in a frame of elaborate scrolls that links a semidome over the window to the frame of the central rectangle. An enlargement of a panel in the semidome has a cherub standing on a basin while balancing a basket of fruit on its head; this is Cupid playing canephorus, a youth or a maiden carrying a basket on the head. In ancient Greece, a canephorus was a maiden who bore on her head a basket of sacred objects at the feasts of Demeter, Bacchus, and Athena. One of the more famous examples of the figure is on the garden terrace of Vignola's Casino at Caprarola, Italy.

In addition, there are irregularly shaped panels with rinceaux ending in the head of an heraldic eagle. A rectangular panel is enlivened by a double rinceau ending in a stylized rooster.

No less plentiful is the detail of the cornice and frieze, also of plas-

The semidome over a window bay in the Periodical Room. Note Cupid playing canephorus.

A sunken panel with a swirl of acanthus ending in an eagle head in the ceiling of the Periodical Room.

LEFT. Portion of the semidome over the window bay, showing Cupid as canephorus between rinceaux ending in dolphins.

A panel in the first section of the Periodical Room.

A rooster rising from a pair of rinceaux on the ceiling of the Periodical Room.

ter stained to resemble wood. The abundance of ornament in the form of lion masks, fruit swags, and enriched modillions and the deep relief of the detail make the ceiling so effective.

On the walls, at eye level and framed by fluted pilasters are panels in low relief carved in French walnut. They repeat three familiar patterns: fruit garlands, scroll frames, and fluttering ribbons.

To light the room are large bronze chandeliers with the familiar ornament of acanthus, bayleaf wreath with ribbon, bearded lion mask, and cartouche on a scroll frame. The gold finish is in "electro gold," but "mercury gold" was the actual specification. With time, the finish darkened and the old patina was brought back during the room's restoration in 1983. The brass bucket, a reflector, is at the center, a modern touch dating also from 1983, as are the clear glass bulbs. The lighting is controlled by dimmers.

Beneath the chandeliers are the tables, which are works of art in

A lion mask on a chandelier in the Periodical Room.

themselves. They are 22 feet long and 4 feet wide. Their veneer is of oak with a border consisting of two strips of ebony crossbanded in Carpathian elm burr and, enframing the whole, is a curved oak border with a relief of scales. Set in the burr are bits of ebony in the shape of squares and rectangles with rounded ends.

The tables are called trestletable because the pedestals are braced by a horizontal piece. On the outer sides of the pedestals, at the center, are the arms of the City of New York. It is a variation on the official seal in that the seaman on the left wears different clothes and the Indian on the right has a somewhat different pose. To either side of the center are volutes adorned with sprays of bay and imbricated bezants or flat disks. The volutes have bases ending in dolphin heads. The pedestals rest on blocks of Verde Antique from Roxbury, Vermont. The tables were made by the Derby Desk Company of Boston, with the carving credited to Michael Zawislan.

The table lamps, which will be examined in detail in the Main Reading Room on the third floor, are the Library's own, designed by Carrère & Hastings. They are of bronze with a bright copper shade. The outside of the shades was originally painted sea-green, as they are elsewhere in the Library; the ones here had the paint removed from the outside and the stand brightened in 1983. Originally the stand had a dark finish.

The chairs, made by the Marble & Shattuck Chair Company of Cleveland, Ohio, are one of several types designed by the architects.

MICHAEL ZAWISLAN, wood carver, 1885–1975. Born in Poland. Came to the United States in 1910 and worked for the Derby Desk Company of Boston. Became the design carver at Steinway & Son, the piano maker.

The coat of arms of New York City on the table pedestal in the Periodical Room.

Official seal of the City of New York. Courtesy Museum of the City of New York.

Dolphin head of a table pedestal in the Periodical Room. The marble below is Verde Antique from Roxbury, Vermont.

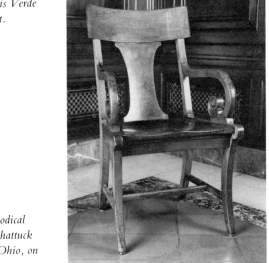

A walnut wood chair in the Periodical Room, made by the Marble & Shattuck Chair Company of Cleveland, Ohio, on the design of Carrère & Hastings.

In this magnificent setting are murals painted on canvas, depicting the buildings of leading New York publishers of books, magazines, and newspapers. Installed in 1983, the murals were executed from photographs by Richard Haas, who was assisted by Jonathan Williams, Jill Steinberg, and Louise Hamlan.

Starting at the right of the entrance door is the building of Charles Scribner and Sons at 597 Fifth Avenue. The firm was family-owned until it merged in 1984 with Macmillan, Inc. The building was designed by Ernest Flagg, the architect of the United States Naval Academy in Annapolis, Maryland. Next is the former building of McGraw-Hill, on West 42nd Street, an early Modernistic skyscraper. It is the work of Raymond Hood, Godley and Fouilhoux. The Hearst Building, third on the north wall, is the headquarters of the publishing corporation founded by William Randolph Hearst, who was the nation's most important newspaper publisher from 1910 to 1935. The building is the work of Joseph Urban, the theatrical designer best known for the sets he made for the Ziegfeld Follies.

Tucked away above the pediment of the door leading to the next room is a partial view of the headquarters of *The Reader's Digest,* founded by DeWitt and Lila Acheson Wallace. Today this extraordinary magazine has a worldwide circulation of over 30,000,000 and is published in forty-one editions and seventeen languages. The building, which is in Pleasantville, Westchester County, New York, was designed by James C. Mackenzie.

To the right of the same door is the Look Building, on the northwest corner of Madison Avenue and 51st Street. It was once the headquarters of Cowles Communications, which originated in Des Moines, Iowa, and, for years, was the publisher of *Look,* an illustrated magazine of wide circulation.

Historically the most interesting canvases are on the east wall with the views of Newspaper Row; that cluster of newspapers occupied the south side of Park Row across from City Hall for several generations. The panel to the left of the window has City Hall conspicuously in the foreground to the left. Beyond it, to the right, are seen the buildings of Joseph Pulitzer's *World,* of Charles Anderson Dana's *Sun,* the *Tribune* of Whitelaw Reid, heir of Horace Greeley, and, in the same building, William Randolph Hearst's *Journal,* later the *Journal-American,* and, last, the *Times* of Adolph Ochs Sulzberger's *New York Times* before the newspaper moved to Times Square. Anyone reading about our country, the city, and newspaper publishing around 1900 should have this view before him. The fierce competition among the newspapers was obviously exacerbated by propinquity. The big struggle was between Pulitzer and Hearst, and they were only several hundred feet apart. The mural to the right shows the earlier home of the *Times* about the year Sulzberger bought it. The old Post Office on the far right stood in the south triangle of City Hall Park before it was torn down in 1929. The statue of Benjamin Franklin shown in front of the *Times* building is now in City Hall Park.

As to the buildings themselves, the best known was the *Tribune* building, designed by Richard Morris Hunt, architect of the base of the Statue of Liberty and the central wing of the Metropolitan Museum of Art. In the 1880s, it was the city's tallest building.

On the south wall is the Puck Building, which stands at 295–305 Lafayette Street on East Houston Street. Here, *Puck,* a satirical illustrated weekly, was published. Its founder was Joseph Keppler, a Viennese who came to New York via St. Louis and first worked for *Frank Leslie's Illustrated Newspaper.* In 1876, he founded his magazine, *Puck, Humoristiches Wochenblatt,* a German-language

weekly, for the city's German population. The English edition appeared a year later and lasted until 1918.

In the middle of the wall is a view of the Harper & Bros. Building, which once stood at the corner of Pearl Street and Franklin Square, directly south of the Brooklyn Bridge. This famous publisher, now Harper & Row, was founded by James Harper, who was mayor of New York City in 1844–1845.

The *Evening Post,* ancestor of the *New York Post,* is the subject of the third canvas on the south wall. This is one of its old buildings, still standing at 20 Vesey Street. Founded in 1801 by Alexander Hamilton, the paper was once owned by the poet William Cullen Bryant, for whom Bryant Park is named, and John Bigelow who, as first president of the New York Public Library, played so important a role in its founding and in bringing about the construction of the Library building.

The first mural on the west wall shows the *Herald* Building, which formerly stood on the block bounded by Broadway, Sixth Avenue, and 35th and 36th Streets. The newspaper was founded by the Scot James Gordon Bennett who left it to his son, James Gordon Bennett, Jr. The latter is best known for having founded *The Paris Herald,* today the *International Herald Tribune.* It was he who commissioned the firm of McKim, Mead & White to design the building depicted. The daily newspaper was the first to move uptown from Park Row and it provided the name for the square on which its building stood, famous for the presence of Macy's Department Store and the song of George M. Cohan which goes "Give my regards to Broadway/ Remember me to Herald Square . . ."

Also on the west wall is the old *Times* Building on Times Square; it was designed by Cyrus L. W. Eidlitz. The newspaper moved here from Park Row in 1904 and remained in the building until it moved to its present address at 229

West 43rd Street. Although the *Times* was founded in 1851, its rise to importance came with its purchase in 1896 by Adolph Simon Sulzberger. The son of German-Jewish immigrants, the newspaper publisher began his publishing career in 1878 with the *Chattanooga Times.* He then moved to New York and ran his newly purchased daily until his death in 1935.

The third and last mural on the west wall is of the Time-Life Building, built in 1938 as part of Rockefeller Center. *Time,* the weekly news magazine, was started in March 1923, by Briton Hadden and Henry Robinson Luce. The magazine was a success from the start. With Hadden's death in 1929, Luce took over and established what is today one of the nation's larger publishing empires. Among its publications are *Fortune, Life,* and *People.* The building is the work of a team called Associated Architects, the best known of whom were Harvey Willey Corbett, Raymond Hood, and Wallace K. Harrison.

Off the first room is one that faces Fifth Avenue. Its doorway, on its south side, has a duplicate of the Formosa marble frame and pediment seen on the entrance doorway. On the north side, in Rouge jaspe marble from near Toulon, France, is a pediment resting on an entablature with a pulvinated frieze.

The second room of the Periodical Room.

It will be noticed that the marble frame of both doorways is very bright. This finish was given to the marble in the course of the restoration undertaken in 1982. The Rouge jaspe, with the customary polish, can be seen in the base running around the room. In the floor, framing the Welsh quarry tiles, are bands of Red Champlain and Hauteville.

The ceiling above is in imitation wood with very little ornament, save for rosettes. What is to be noticed here is the beautiful paneling around the walls, even on the deep reveals of the windows. The

Panel of the second room of the Periodical Room, with heads of dogs and griffons and at the top a winged cherub head with two birds.

Panel of the second room of the Periodical Room with a satyr mask, lion heads, birds, and acanthus.

Panel of the second room of the Periodical Room with a cartouche ringed with sphinxes, a winged cherub head, a crouching nymph, dog heads, and birds.

Panel of the second room of the Periodical Room with a cartouche ringed with sphinxes, a winged cherub head, a crouching nymph, dog heads, and birds.

paneling of the first room is impressive enough; this is even more so, especially in the variety of the basic eight patterns that are repeated on the French walnut. Their design has one common theme: a center consisting of a cartouche on a scroll frame. The variations take the shape of satyr masks, winged cherub heads, lion heads, dog heads, real and fanciful birds, sphinxes, and cornucopia, along with the ever present acanthus in myriad forms. The inspiration is probably 16th century French classical such as seen in the paneling from the Château de Gaillon, now in the Metropolitan Museum of Art.

Possible inspiration for the Library panels was an oak panel from the chapel of the Château de Gaillon, ca. 1510, near Rouen, France. Bequest of George Blumenthal, Metropolitan Museum of Art.

Bronze work, found in the lamps and the chandeliers, is also seen in the railing at the Delivery Desk and the gallery above. At the base of the wall near the door is a register screen. Even this modest screen has a grid of squares with rosettes at the crossings, acanthus leaves in the corners, circles of the metal, and curved bits in the corners, which end in volutes.

On the far, north, wall are two drawings by Richard Haas. The left shows a bearded man, who represents scholarship and the right, a woman and child who are symbols for education.

In these two rooms, readers can obtain any one of 10,000 current periodicals, published in twenty-two languages in 124 countries. Eleven hundred of them are purchased in microfilm; 450 are microfilmed by the Library. What is awesome is not simply the sheer quantity of these publications, but their ready availability to all. We have called the Library "a people's palace." That epithet is underscored in every way by these two rooms.

A few newspapers can be obtained, on microfilm, in the north part of the Main Reading Room. Most of them are in the Newspaper Division in the Annex at 521 West 43rd Street.

On leaving the DeWitt Wallace Periodical Room, our tour takes us once again along the great 326-foot gallery of the first floor. The gallery goes all the way north to the Map Division in Room 117. Here is a duplication of Room 108, with a few changes brought about by time and use. The chandeliers have the dark finish that they have had for years and they do not have the modern reflectors. The table lamps have given way to a modern table-length reflector with fluorescent lighting, which was installed in 1967. The walnut chairs are original. The tables are of the same design as those in Room 108, but the veneer or marquetry is different. The center rectangles of the tables are of walnut, with frames of Carpathian Elm burr with its knotty pattern, ebony, and oak.

The Map Division claims that it is the most used public map collection in the world. And well it might be. Aside from the large quantity of maps, there are more than 6,000 atlases and more than 11,000 books. Of particular interest are the early maps of American cities and towns.

Outside the Map Division there is ample light to examine the doorway and the arched bay of which it is a part.

Opposite the doorway is a corridor leading to Room 121, the Science and Technology Research Center. The garlanded overdoors here set off the jointing and the scale of the white marble walls, which rise to an appropriately elaborate cornice. Above the cornice of the

The second room of the Periodical Room. The posts of the bronze railing are treated as double balusters.

In the same room, the upper rail of the bronze railing of the Delivery Desk has a Greek key with rosette.

A register screen in the Periodical Room.

The Map Division, Room 117.

doorway to Room 121 is a circular niche containing the bust of the Emperor Antoninus Pius with a similar niche above a nearby door having the bust of the Emperor Hadrian. Both are by Leone Clerici, who did the busts in the center of the South–North Gallery.

Although Room 121 lacks the ornamental opulence of the Map Division and the DeWitt Wallace Periodical Room, it has the same types of tables and chairs. Only the veneer of the tables and the shape of the chairs are different; the chairs in the other two rooms are square-backed, while the ones here are round-backed. And, also as in the other two rooms, it is wonderfully lit, with its row of high windows looking out on 42nd Street.

The Science and Technology Research Center has seen the genesis of many scientific and technological triumphs. Several come to mind. Here Chester Carlson did the research for his heliography, he developed into the Xerox machine, the first of many copying machines. Edwin Land combed through books and scientific publications here in the research that led to his inventing the Polaroid camera.

Nearby are the stair landing and elevator bank that serve the secondary entrance to the Library on 42nd Street. It is described in chapter XVII, The 42nd Street Staircase.

Before returning to Astor Hall, we stop at the north end of the South–North Gallery to look south. What an extraordinary corridor it is! There is nothing like it in the country.

An overdoor in the hall leading to the Science and Technology Research Center. The same panel exists elsewhere on the first floor and can be seen in the corridor leading to the Trustees' Room on the second floor.

OPPOSITE. *View south from the north end of the South-North Gallery. The elevator bank is on the right.*

THE NORTH STAIRWAY AND THE SLAVONIC (Rooms 216 and 217), THE ORIENTAL (Room 219) AND THE ECONOMICS AND PUBLIC AFFAIRS DIVISIONS (Room 228) SECOND FLOOR GALLERY

BEFORE MOUNTING THE NORTH STAIRS, it is worth standing back in Astor Hall to examine them. What we see beneath the stairs with its railing is a complete arch in itself, actually a seventeen-foot rampant arch. The arch is called rampant because one impost, or arch end, is higher than the other. At first, the architects wanted the arch and steps above to be made of single pieces of stone. The impracticality of such construction became obvious. It was inevitable that the treads of the steps would wear away with time and have to be replace. The solution, as seen here, was to have arch and steps made separately.

The railing consists of an upper and lower rail between which is stone with oblong openings with round ends. The openings are framed by a guilloche with alternating circles and oblongs; the spaces between are filled with acanthus and flowers. Beneath the rail is a Greek key band.

The triumphant note, the note of celebration, echoes at the very start of the climb; the low, massive, curved railing that serves as newel post, beautifully enriched by acanthus and oakleaf. What is particularly successful is the large rosette from which spring acanthus leaves that end in flowers.

We mount the steps to a square landing with a barrel vault of marble, for all is marble in or next to Astor Hall. Set in the two walls, which are at right angles, are blind arch bays. In the one on the right is the bronze bust of John Merven Carrère by Jo Davidson. In the other is a marble plaque of recent date that reads:

OPPOSITE. *The North Stairway at Astor Hall.*

The North Stairway railing showing the open guilloche with rosette, acanthus, flowers, and olives.

The massive curved railing enriched with acanthus and oakleaf.

OPPOSITE. *The bust of John Merven Carrère by Jo Davidson.*

NEW YORK PUBLIC LIBRARY
(the Library seal)
ASTOR LENOX
AND TILDEN
FOUNDATIONS
ASTOR HALL
NAMED IN RECOGNITION OF
THE ASTOR FAMILY
WHOSE GENEROSITY AND DEVOTION
TO THIS LIBRARY
OVER FIVE GENERATIONS
ARE EXEMPLIFIED IN OUR TIME BY
BROOKE RUSSELL ASTOR
TRUSTEE
MAY 18, 1978

Set in the bays at the landing are benches with sides decorated by grotesque reliefs of satyr masks.

Plaque in recognition of Brooke Russell Astor.

JOHN M. CARRÈRE

A grotesque on the bench at the first landing of the North Stairway—a satyr mask crowned with ivy and a mouth filled with stylized bay leaf and bayberry.

Overhead is a *lanterne d'escalier,* or stair light, which is contrasted with the globe lanterns of the South-North Gallery and the bronze chandeliers of various rooms. This sumptuous lantern one is of eighteenth-century French inspiration, quite obviously designed by Carrère & Hastings, and it is yet another example of the attention to detail and of the care lavished on the building by the firm. It is about as fine a lantern as any and could take its place beside an ancestor, the stairwell lantern of the Petit Trianon at Versailles, designed by Ange-Jacques Gabriel.

As we have noticed, the handling of the stone, both on the interior and the exterior of the Library, has hardly been limited to enrichment. Architectural devices abound, particularly in the use of stereotomy. In the blind bay holding the plaque honoring Brooke Russell Astor, the arch above consists of splayed, stepped voussoirs. The marble here, as in Astor Hall, is Dorset/Danby.

The bay is repeated on the wall along the stairs. Overhead, sloping upward, is a barrel vault divided by transverse arches, a reminder that grand staircases always have equally grand vaults.

On the wall at this point is a portrait of John Jacob Astor by Edward Dalton Marchant, painted in 1836. The real estate magnate and bibliophile was sixty-seven at the time.

Before coming to the second floor, we turn to look at the interplay of space that is so much a part of the wonder of this building. Its match in the city can be found only in the Great Hall of the Cunard Building at 25 Broadway, where Thomas Hastings served as consultant, the Metropolitan Museum of Art, and the Low Library of Columbia University.

At the second floor, really a mezzanine or entresole, it is worth turning left to stop beneath one of the bay arches overlooking Astor Hall. Here is yet another view of the marble room, and here we can obtain a close inspection of the ceiling.

The railing here may come as something of a surprise, as it is uncommonly low, being only 2 feet 6¼ inches, as compared to the 3-foot height of the stair railing. The explanation for this lies in the difficulty the architects had in matching the scale of the railing to the inside of the arch. Had it been of standard height, at least three feet, it would have looked far too high from below. Carrère & Hastings simply lowered it so that it would be in visual proportion to the arch.

The corridor to the south leads to the executive offices, which will be seen later. Part way to the south, a corridor goes west. It leads to the Slavonic Division, in Rooms 216 and 217. The division collects

The lantern over the first landing of the North Stairway.

OPPOSITE. View of Astor Hall from the North Stairway.

OPPOSITE LEFT. *The view through the central bay of Astor Hall down 41st Street from the Second Floor Gallery.*

OPPOSITE RIGHT. *The view through the north bay of Astor Hall to the north side of the portico.*

View of Astor Hall and the South Stairway from the Second Floor Gallery.

Astor Hall from the Second Floor Gallery looking east. It should be pointed out this view and the two following were taken before the bronze globes were installed in the portico in 1985.

OPPOSITE BELOW. *The low railing of the Second Floor Gallery.*

material in twelve Slavonic languages and in Latvian and Lithuanian. More than 750 periodicals and 120 newspapers come here in the course of the year. Opposite the Slavonic Division, in Rooms 219, 221, and 223, is the Oriental Division. More than 100 Oriental languages are represented. In addition to books, there is a continually expanding list of journals and newspapers. At the end of the corridor, to the north, is the Economic and Public Affairs Division, in Room 228, which boasts a vast collection of publications of international agencies and of governments throughout the world. This is one of the largest and most-used divisions in the Library. Part way north to the Economics Division, in the east marble wall, is a shallow niche with a drinking fountain. The chief ornament is a bronze lion mask originally with its mouth as a spout. (The lion mask is now made sanitary by having the water piped to a special spout and a shallow enamel cup.) The niche wall is of Breccia Violette, from Tuscany, with insets of Belgian Black, from Mazy near Namur, Belgium. A dolphin in relief is seen on the keystone of the niche's flat arch, while the basin rests on acanthus leaves revolving into rinceaux and rosettes.

A lion mask of bronze at the drinking fountain of the Second Floor Gallery.

The flat walls of Pentelic marble serve a useful purpose here; they are a place for exhibiting some of the Library's treasures, notably those to do with the city. A frequently exhibited object is the landmark Commissioners' Map of the 1811, which gave Manhattan its famous grid.

Before ascending the stairs to the third floor, we may pause to appreciate the stairway itself. Monumental stairways are usually confined to one floor; this one links three. In addition, Carrère & Hastings had to assure circulation on the second floor by another south-north corridor. We have seen the architects' skillful handling of decoration and the use of, for example, stone in the stereotomic vault of Astor Hall, and we have inevitably become aware of them as masters of planning as well.

We return to the North Stairway and go up a few steps to a landing. The landing is square in plan with chamfered corners, or an octagon with four wide sides divided by four narrow ones. On stepping into this landing, we pass beneath a segmental arch, over which is an open bay with the north corridor of the third floor beyond. This bay, round-arched, is one of the four shaping the top part of the landing. The second bay, to the north, is blind. The third to the west has a square-arched doorway opening on a shallow balcony. The doorway is framed by a wide panel bordered by a cyma reversa with egg-and-dart. The voluted keystone of the square arch joins a course above, beneath which is an egg-and-dart ovolo. Above is the

The catfish and cattails on the keystone of the drinking fountain of the Second Floor Gallery.

The drinking fountain of the Second Floor Gallery.

familiar railing seen at the first flight of stairs, but here it has no open work. The rest of the bay is glazed.

Through the doorway we can see the north courtyard with a view of the high windows of the third floor. They are the windows of the Main Reading Room. They have a nobility and a grandeur that would have appealed to Piranesi or Hubert Robert, especially at night. The bronze door itself is up to the customary standard of Carrère & Hastings. We come on another lever handle here. This one might be called the *PL* because of the two letters found on an oval cabuchon set in a pearl frame. Around it are sprays of acanthus, bound by ribbon, that extend to enclose a pair of rosettes and a small vase in relief. The head has a sunken panel with a rosette of acanthus, while, extending from the same head, is a knob shaped by godroons. Another of the *PL* handles will be found at the Trustees' Room; it is easier to see the details on that one.

The fourth, or south, bay is fully open. Here the architects placed the second portion of the stairway, the part going to the third floor.

In this area, the lower part of the walls is rusticated, which is necessitated by the use of stone. Were there not the sunken channels, the walls would be bland and possibly oppressive. For the same reason the architects linked the walls with a course bearing an egg-and-dart to give form to the surface and to divide the walls horizontally.

The architects also repeated the marble stairway railing in the open bay to the east. This time they did not have to reduce the railing height, as the open bay is high enough, whereas the arch of the bay on the second floor was too low, forcing the architects to shrink the railing.

Overhead, the dome is shaped by the octagon below. From the narrow sides rise curved panels embellished with trophies in relief. The panels form two matching pairs on the diagonal. One pair has the attributes of the arts, an Ionic capital, the head of Minerva in relief, and the artist's palette and brushes; the whole is decorated with sprigs of bay and oak. The other pair portrays science and industry, with such symbols as a globe, an anchor, a rudder, a hammer, and an open book with curling parchment and quills. Above them are four more, smaller panels with clusters of hanging fruit.

Between the panels, above the arches of the wide sides of the octagon, are four large additional ones. They, too, bear trophies showing musical instruments (Music); elaborate urns, a hammer, the Belvedere Torso, and carved vases (Sculpture); a palette, brushes, and an easel (Painting); and a Corinthian capital, ruler, T square, and compass (Architecture). At the top, the panels are joined by swags of

The lever handle of the door overlooking the north court.

The dome of the landing of the North Stairway at the Second Floor Gallery.

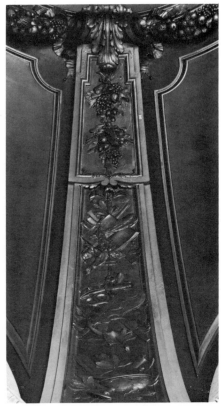

A dome panel, Science and Industry, with an open book, Mercury's winged helmet, a rudder, an anchor, and a globe.

fruit that hang from volutes, each one of which is covered with acanthus. In the center of the swags with fluttering ribbons are satyr masks from which the trophies seem to hang. The top of the dome has a circular torus of bay leaves and bayberries within which there is a small saucer dome of grooves, with stopped fluting and a patera of acanthus leaves. The ground of the main dome is a soft raspberry red with the detail picked out in gold.

From the patera is suspended another of those Carrère & Hastings stairway lanterns executed in the highest 18th-century manner although, in that century, the lantern would have been gilded. The best spot to examine the lantern detail is from the third floor corridor. Volutes, guilloches, Vitruvian wave, rosettes, acanthus in husks, fruit swags, and even eagles are on it.

At first, the architects intended to have a dome of stone. Happily, they changed their minds and opted for stucco. Stucco is a splendid material because it is easy to handle, inexpensive, and subject to any shape. Also, it can be given color.

Trophies suspended from a satyr mask symbolize Sculpture. The Belvedere torso, carved vases, mallet and chisel, and other instruments are seen here along with oak leaves, fluttering ribbons, fruit swags, and bound bay leaves and bayberries.

A satyr mask holding musical instruments.

We proceed up the stairs to the third floor to pause to examine the arch overhead. It consists of two flat bands between which is a sunken panel with octagonal coffering. The coffers are enriched with leaf-and-dart and egg-and-dart and a beautiful rosette.

Next to this arch is another, with splayed voussoirs. Set in the

A rosette on the splayed arch.

The splayed arch at the top of the North Stairway.

The lantern over the second landing of the North Stairway.

soffit of the splayed portion of the voussoirs are nine shallow square coffers, each with acanthus-and-dart and a rosette.

Beneath this second arch the abutments have long vertical recessed panels with a frame consisting of a cyma reversa with acanthus and five-petal flowers.

Just beyond the head of the stairs, to either side, are two magnificent railings of dark bronze. They must be among the most splendid of their kind in the nation and can be compared to the wrought-iron-and-bronze railings of the great stairway in the San Francisco City Hall (designed by Bakewell & Brown). Designed by Carrère & Hastings and cast by the Henry Bonnard Company of Mount Vernon, New York, they are jewellike in their invention and intricacy.

What is fascinating about the railings, other than their beauty, is that, like the terrace flagpoles, they are an encyclopedia of classical ornament. We have already met much detail on our tour and we will meet more. There are the familiar, by now, lion paw and dolphin head, but also to be seen are the ram's head and the swan.

We may pause here after our climb. Just on the stairway alone we have been given a series of visually heightening sensations. We began by studying a giant twisting of acanthus in Astor Hall. Then we viewed the hall, with its variety of perspectives. We paused at the Second Floor Gallery drinking fountain, with a bronze lion mask. On going up the second flight of the North Stairway, we stood in an octagon, which rises to an elaborately adorned dome, and looked out a window across a majestic court. And, now, we find ourselves by a bronze railing of almost unequaled splendor at the Third Floor Landing.

A vase with an upper part with curved channeling and a godroon base. The two handles have satyr masks.

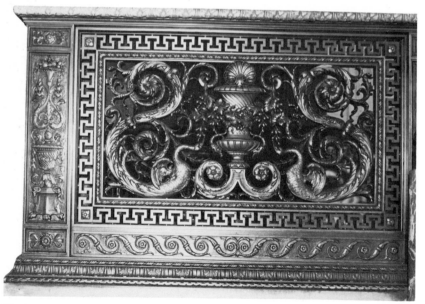

The bronze railing at the top of the North Stairway at the Third Floor Landing. This is a triumphant example of classical ornament.

A vertical panel of the bronze railing. A pair of dolphins serves as support for a fruit- *filled bowl. Note the ram's heads and lion paws of the base.*

RIGHT. View down the North Stairway.

124

IX

THIRD FLOOR LANDING HALL
STOKES GALLERY. BERG EXHIBITION ROOM (Room 318). BERG COLLECTION (Room 320). ARENTS COLLECTIONS (Room 324). PRINT GALLERY. ART REFERENCE ROOM (Room 313). PRINTS, PHOTOGRAPHS AND SPENCER COLLECTION (Room 308). RARE BOOK ROOM (Room 303). EDNA B. SALOMON ROOM (Room 316).

A MARBLE BENCH, like the ones found on the first floor, is at hand for us to sit on, and we can examine, in comfort, the Third Floor Landing Hall which serves as vestibule to the Main Reading Room to the west. Here marble has given way to wood and to stucco in imitation of wood.

As in Astor Hall, we have the magic of symmetry on a grand scale. Equal bays, some blind and some open, are beneath arches. Paired Corinthian pilasters, 17 feet 9 inches high, separate the bays. (Pilaster shafts, it should be noted, do not taper as do those of columns. These here are two feet wide both at the bottom and at the top.) It is wonderful to see how well the functional, so prized in our time, is accommodated in this supremely classical setting. The bays, as in Astor Hall, match. Opposite pairs of bays, the north and south, open to stairs and to corridors. On the east and west sides are opposite trios, with the center bay on the east opening to the Edna B. Salomon Room, Room 316, and its opposite opening to the Catalog Room, part of Room 315. To either side of these are blind bays with murals on canvas by Edward Laning.

The paired pilasters support an entablature that runs around the room without a break. Above it is a large barrel vault of stucco divided into a variety of panels. The central one consists of a large sunken rectangle within which is another rectangle with round ends framed with acanthus, stopped fluting, and a fruit garland. In the corners are

OPPOSITE. *The Third Floor Landing.*

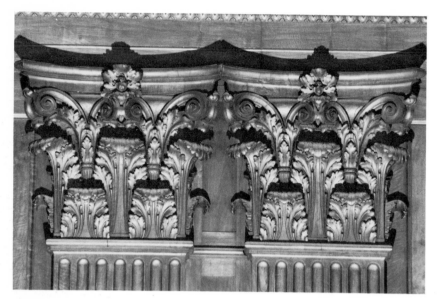

octagons with rosettes, which are also found on the sunken panels. A double guilloche embellishes the frame of the large rectangle, as it does those of the smaller panels.

The barrel vault is open at both ends. This makes possible its extension beyond the main entablature to open glazed bays.

The visitor will easily recognize the varieties of marble on the floor. Hauteville with borders of Gray Siena take up most of the space, supplemented by a band of Lake Champlain "Oriental Variety." The wall base around the room is of the now familiar Rouge Jaspe.

The doorways of Rooms 315 and 316, which are directly opposite each other, are magnificent. Each is framed by a band of moldings which, at the top, form crossettes. Above, each has a modillion cornice supported by volute ancones. A dentil band links the upper volutes of the two ancones, and beneath it is a pulvinated frieze embellished with imbricated bay leaves and bayberries. Above is a lunette with one of Edward Laning's canvases, while, at the top of the lunette arch, a voluted keystone of wood has sprays of laurel, as do all the arches in the room.

Edward Laning executed the murals between 1938 and 1942 as part of a Works Progress Administration (WPA) Project with supplies furnished by Isaac Newton Phelps Stokes, author of the *Iconography of Manhattan Island* and a great patron of the Library. Laning depicted the story of the recorded word. The first mural, to the left of the entrance to the Catalog Room (Room 315), shows Moses descending from Mount Sinai with the Ten Commandments, "the

EDWARD LANING, painter, 1906–1981. Born in Petersburg, Illinois, he studied painting at the school of the Art Institute of Chicago and at the Art Students League. He taught at the League for many years as well as at the Cooper Union and the National Academy School of Fine Arts. His mural work is to be found in the Abraham Lincoln High School in Brooklyn and in the Manhattan Savings Bank as well as in post offices and hotels across the country.

Writing was the Writing of God, graven on tablets." Beneath the prophet, the Children of Israel are dancing and are worshipping the Golden Calf. In the second mural, to the right of the same door, a monk of the Middle Ages is copying a manuscript while, behind him, is a scene of destruction and rapine. In the third, to the left of the doorway to Room 316, Johann Gutenberg shows a proof of his Bible to Adolph of Nassau, Elector of Mainz. The fourth, to the right, represents America's contribution, Ottmar Mergenthaler at the keyboard of his linotype machine as his patron, Whitelaw Reid of the New York *Tribune,* examines a page printed by the new device, while behind him is the Brooklyn Bridge and, nearby, a newsboy shouting the headlines. In the lunette over the roor to Room 316, a student reads beneath a tree, and opposite, over the door of Room 315, a mother reads to her son. Overhead, in the vault, Prometheus brings to mankind fire and knowledge stolen from the gods. The style of the murals is derived from the academic naturalism, or realism, made popular in Paris in the last century.

Serving as climax to the splendid room are four more of the magnificent marble lamp standards that were first seen in Astor Hall. Even the bench reminds us again of the ornamental wealth of the classical. Inevitably, this antechamber, for such it is, recalls a sacristy of a great Italian church or a great room by the French architect Ange-Jacques Gabriel, or even the sacristy in the opera *Manon.* Here, wood is used on an unparalleled scale. Marble, wood, stucco, the bronze railings, the lamp standards all place the room in a category of its own.

Off this mighty antechamber are square foyers to the north and south corridors. In design they actually form part of the domed landings of the stairways. Their purpose, however, is to serve as a transition in and out of the great hall. On three sides are three similar arches with posts faced with sunken panels. In the soffit of the arch are square coffers with rosettes. Both the sunken panels of the posts and the arch coffers are framed with leaf-and-flower.

Inside the bay opening on the corridor is an archway framed with large leaf-and-flower (the flower replaces the dart) on a cyma reversa, which is more elaborate than those also to be seen on the panels. Overhead is a tympanum with a sunken bowl containing the bust of Victory crowned with a wreath of oak leaves. It is the work of Christian Daniel Rauch, 1777–1857, a German sculptor, famous especially for his equestrian statue Frederick the Great, in Berlin, and a much-reproduced statue of Goethe in a long coat. The bust rests on a volute that links the bowl, the tympanum, and the door frame.

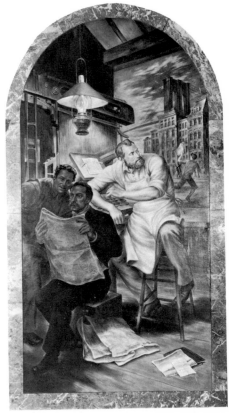

One of the murals by Edward Laning. This one depicts Ottmar Mergenthaler and his typemaking machine with Whitelaw Reid of The New York Tribune *studying the results of mechanical typesetting. Courtesy* The New York Public Library, Astor, Lenox and Tilden Foundations.

The pedestal of one of the benches on the Third Floor Landing. Acanthus, a pair of dolphins, and a pair of double volutes ending in lion paws are in relief.

The open bay looks over the stair landing and across, through the arched window, to the north court. It permits yet another view of the high arched windows of the Main Reading Room. The window frame consists of rusticated sides and voussoirs, both with a curved chamfer.

The corridor beyond is the Stokes Gallery, named for Isaac Newton Phelps Stokes. For many years a Library trustee, he gave the Library his great collection of views of American cities and towns, the most important being those of New York. Now in the Prints, Photographs and Spencer Collection, they are periodically shown on these walls.

The door at hand is the entrance to Room 318, the Berg Exhibition Room, where manuscripts and rare books are displayed. The ceiling here has a cove, the curved edge of the ceiling that links it to the wall. The first we have met on the tour, it is a device, as Edith Wharton and Ogden Codman, Jr., tell us in *The Decoration of Houses* (in this Series) that "greatly increases the apparent height in a low-studded room." The doorway, on the room side, has a marble frame of Rouge Jaspe with moldings and crossettes. In addition to a cornice and a frieze, it has a round pediment.

Room 320 (visited only by special permission) houses the Berg Collection of English and American Literature. The collection consists of first editions, manuscripts, and letters. The room was installed in 1940 according to the designs of Eggers & Higgins, heirs to the practice of John Russell Pope. The style is English classical and it has some enrichment. The work of T. S. Eliot, Virginia Woolf, Charles Dickens, and others are represented in this collection. A portrait of William Makepeace Thackery and a desk that once belonged to Dickens emphasize the English presence. A good portion of the collection, along with the room paneling and the objects, was given by Dr. Albert A. Berg in memory of his brother, Dr. Henry W. Berg. Owen D. Young, who for many years was at the head of General Electric Company, was another major donor.

In Room 322 is the Arents Collection (visited only by special permission). The room and collection were given by George Arents (1875–1960), who made his fortune in tobacco. The collection consists largely of books, manuscripts, letters, and other items related to tobacco and going back to 1507. The interior is the work of Aymar Embury II, who did the sign stands on the Terrace. It, too, is English classical, although without the enrichment found on the moldings of its Berg neighbor. The chimney breast on the south wall is eighteenth-century work.

The bust of Victory by Christian Daniel Rauch above the arch of the north foyer leading to the Stokes Gallery.

The Berg Exhibition Room—Room 318.

We now go directly to the south corridor. Its foyer duplicates the one to the north. The bust in the sunken bowl above the door is that of the wreath-crowned Napoleon by Raimondo Trentanove, 1792–1832, commissioned by James Lenox.

At this place we can turn to look at the dome over the South Stairway, a twin of the dome to the north. Beyond is Room 313, the Art Reference Room. The corridor is called the Print Gallery; throughout the year, prints from the Library's excellent collection are placed on view. At the end of the Print Gallery, to the left, is the Print Room, Room 308, which holds the Prints, Photographs and Spencer Collection. (It is visited only by special permission.) A second corridor goes west at this point. The door to Room 303, the Rare Book Room (visited only by special permission), is on the left. Among the rare books and manuscripts is Jefferson's handwritten copy of the Declaration of Independence.

We go back to the Third Floor Landing to Room 316, the Edna

The marble doorways and bronze doors of the Edna B. Salomon Room, Room 316, and the Catalog Room, Room 315, are identical. The photograph depicts the door to the Catalog Room. The only difference is in the door handles; the one shown here is plain, whereas those of the Salomon Room door are enriched.

B. Salomon Room. Formerly devoted to Photographic Services, it has been returned to its original purpose, that of an exhibition hall, and it also serves as the Office of Special Collections. Its monumental doorway is most suitable to that purpose. It has a bronze door of two leaves, each consisting of five square panels with rosettes of acanthus. The panels are framed by bead-and-reel and cyma reversa in acanthus. Surrounding all five panels is a band of arabesques with cabuchons in scroll frames, anthemia, and rosettes. One last frame for the whole leaf is a torus of bay leaf and bayberry. The panel of diamond points at the bottom of each leaf should not be overlooked.

One curiosity is the astragal on the left leaf or fold of the door. An astragal, the word ordinarily identifies a half-round molding on a classical column, is the molded strip applied to one side of a door leaf where the two leaves meet. It projects over the edge in order to overlap the adjoining leaf when the door is closed. The astragal here is a modified Corinthian column with a tiny capital and an elongated fluted shaft almost the door's full length.

As might be expected, the lever handle has not been neglected. This is the third such handle we have seen so far. It might be called the "dolphin" because it boasts a pair of dolphins, as well as a vase of fruit on one side.

The doorway, of Rouge Jaspe, is in the Roman manner. The interior frame consists of a bolection molding, a type of molding, often elaborate, which projects from a flat surface; at the top of the frame there are crossettes. A cornice with modillions rests on ancones. The doorway on the inside of the Edna B. Salomon Room, is also of Rouge Jaspe and has a wholly different treatment. It is, in fact, an aedicule in Roman mutulary Doric, a mutule being one of a series of flat blocks projecting from the soffit of a Doric cornice. The free-standing fluted columns have capitals with an echinus in egg-and-dart and necking with rosettes.

The shaft of the columns is 1 foot 4 inches in diameter and the column height is 10 feet 6 inches, making the ratio the customary 8:1. The diameter at the top is 1 foot 2 inches.

The ceiling, too, has its share of ornament. The cove, which, as we know, adds to a ceiling's height, has toruses enriched with fruit, bands of arabesques, ovolo in egg-and-dart, cyma reversa with acanthus, and even scroll frames. The cove rests on a modified entablature with a frieze adorned with a Greek key band.

Two doors at either end of the room are of Rouge Jaspe marble, to match the entrance off the Third Floor Landing. Instead of a standard pediment, we find round pediments resting on brackets. The walls are covered with a yellow cloth with a small repeat pattern.

The majority of the Library's picture and sculpture collection has been united in the gallery. Most of them were part of the library of James Lenox and came to the Library on its founding. There are four portraits alone of George Washington, one by James Peale, another by Rembrandt Peale, and two by Gilbert Stuart, one standing and one seated. Samuel F. B. Morse is represented by a study of the head

The "dolphin" lever handle of the door to the Edna B. Salomon Room.

The Doric doorway inside the Edna B. Salomon Room.

of Lafayette painted when the artist was working on the famous full-length portrait of the Frenchman, which now hangs in the City Council Chamber in the New York City Hall. Pictures by John Singleton Copley, Sir Joshua Reynolds, and Sir Henry Raeburn are to be found

The Blind Milton Dictating Paradise Lost *to His Daughters* by Mikhaly Munkacsy. *Courtesy The New York Public Library, Astor, Lenox and Tilden Foundations.*

here. Later portraits include one of John Quinn, patron of the avant-garde of the 1900s and 1910s, by Augustus John.

The most familiar to the Library public are, however, three others. The first is the famous *The Blind Milton Dictating* Paradise Lost *to His Daughters* by Mihaly Munkacsy. We know it well from its being reproduced in countless anthologies and collections of poetry. It hung for years in the second floor landing of the North Stairway. The second is Asher B. Durand's *Kindred Spirits,* with William Cullen Bryant and the painter Thomas Cole shown exploring the Catskills. It formerly was on a wall on one of the Third Floor Galleries. A third is the portrait of Mrs. Henry Draper by John W. Alexander, a leading portraitist of the turn of the century. A devoted patron of the Library, Mrs. Draper left a fund to help staff members who, when ill, needed financial assistance. It formerly hung on the second floor landing of the South Stairway.

OPPOSITE. Kindred Spirits, *by Asher B. Durand. The poet William Cullen Bryant and the painter Thomas Cole in the Catskills. Courtesy The New York Public Library, Astor, Lenox and Tilden Foundations.*

Mrs. Henry Draper, a patron of the Library, by John W. Alexander. Courtesy The New York Public Library Astor, Lenox and Tilden Foundations.

From the Edna B. Salomon Room we go across the great ante-chamber, that is, the Third Floor Landing, to the Catalog Room, part of Room 315, the initiation to the great climax of the Library's visual feast.

X

CATALOG ROOM (Room 315)

On entering Room 315 we are in the Catalog Room, which, it might be said, is a second, brightly lit, antechamber to the Main Reading Room beyond it. Here the reader begins the process of obtaining books. Where, until recently, there were card trays around the room, there are now book catalogs listing authors and titles. In addition, computers have been installed on the tables to provide the latest information on the Library's accessions. In the center is now an enlarged Information Desk, and the counter where the reader hands in call slips.

In examining the room, it would be well to start with the doorway, if only to appreciate the contrast between this side of it and the other side, as well as to compare it with the inside of the doorway to Room 316. The Landing Hall side has a frame of Rouge Jaspe; here it is of Hauteville marble and oak. Instead of the pink marble aedicule of Room 316, the door lining has only simple moldings as well as crossettes.

The surrounding wood frame is more elaborate—an announcement that from here on wood is the ruling material. The cornice and the raking cornices of the Doric pediment have mutules, while, between them, the soffits have diamond-shaped frames containing modified rosettes. The pediment is upheld by a pair of ancones with double volutes. On the outside of the ancones are small buttresses, also with double volutes; between the ancones is a frieze in beautiful

OPPOSITE. The Catalog Room prior to its recent transformation.

137

relief, consisting of rinceaux evolving into griffons. Between the rinceaux, above the modern exit sign, is a cartouche in an elaborate scroll frame.

More examples of carved relief are to either side of the doorway. The panel has, at its center, an oval cartouche with a pearl border; on the panel is an arabesque of acanthus and two bunches of grapes. Around the cartouche is a scroll frame topped by an anthemion. At the top of the panel are rinceaux with tendrils ending in dolphin heads. At the bottom, the scroll frame turns into two swirls of acanthus that end in winged sphinxes, each one, like a canephorus, carrying a basket of fruit on its head. A fruit swag links the two fruit baskets.

To the left of the door is a plaque with a profile in relief around which a chaplet reads, "Born A.D. MDCCCXIII, Tablet erected A.D. MCMXIII." Beneath it is the inscription:

TO COMMEMORATE
THE
ONE HUNDREDTH ANNIVERSARY
OF THE BIRTH OF
SIR ISAAC PITMAN
AND IN RECOGNITION OF THE
IMPORTANT COLLECTION OF
SHORTHAND LITERATURE
IN THE
NEW YORK PUBLIC LIBRARY

Even this modest bronze memorial to the man who helped develop present-day shorthand has the necessary classical detail, such as border of egg-and-dart and pearls.

The shelves around the Catalog Room are divided vertically by pilasters with modified Doric capitals, and the pilasters support a modified entablature consisting of cornice with leaf-and-wave molding and a frieze, interrupted above the pilasters, by triglyphs complete with guttae.

On the north and south sides above the lower rows of shelves is a second tier of the same with a walkway behind a bronze railing. The railing has an upper and a lower rail with a Greek key in open work. Between them are thin bronze posts treated as double balusters.

We recognize the flooring, as it consists of the same Welsh quarry tiles found in the DeWitt Wallace Periodical Room and the Map Room. Here, too, are the same low tables with the same pedestals bearing the city's coat of arms. The chairs are different; they are new, purchased in 1972.

The bronze railing that guards the walkway above the shelves. The posts, treated as double balusters, are fixed between upper and lower rails of Greek keys.

XI

MAIN READING ROOM (Room 315)

THE DOORWAY TO the Main Reading Room, like the inside of the doorway of Room 316, takes the form of aedicule, but it is in wood and not in marble. The Doric columns are similarly fluted and have capitals of egg-and-dart; only the necking is adorned with a double guilloche as well as a rosette. Also, the columns are a quarter engaged instead of being freestanding. They support a round pediment with a cornice so spaced that there is room for a panel with an inscription.

The inscription is a passage from Milton's *Areopagitica,* a protest against censorship, written in 1644. To give a fuller understanding, the passage is quoted at length, with the portion on the panel in italics

I know they [books] are as lively, and as vigorously productive as those fabulous Dragons teeth; and being sown up and down, may chance to spring up armed men. And yet on the other hand unless wariness be us'd, as good almost as kill a Man as kill a good Book; who kills a Man kills a reasonable creature, Gods Image; but hee who destroes a good Booke, kills reason it selfe. Many a man lives a burden to the Earth; but *a goode Booke is the pretious life-blood of a master spirit, imbalm'd and treasur'd up on purpose to a life beyond life.*

Beneath the cornice are an egg-and-dart molding and a dentil band. A panel between the capitals contains a pair of rinceaux ending in cherubs. Between the cherubs is a cartouche on a scroll frame. The cherubs remind us again of their importance to Western art.

On the outside of the capitals, set back from them, are volutes with twisting acanthus leaves. Beneath them, on either side of the shafts of the columns, are elaborate wood bars each topped by a modified Corinthian capital. The doorway frame has its ornament, a twisting ribbon that is so spaced that the ribbon bands alternate with acanthus leaves.

The leaves of the door repeat the pattern of the open sides of the doorway; they have wooden bars with modified Corinthian capitals, the same shafts covered with acanthus and cloth-draped urns in relief. Above are two rectangular panels. The topmost, the larger of the two, is sunken and has a round cartouche with an elaborate scroll frame at the center. The panel has a frame in a torus covered with circles, each filled with an open leaf and each joined to the other by a short band. The lower panel has a bearded male mask with two dolphins.

Below the door bars are two more panels. The first one is a short panel with rinceaux, the second with a rectangular shield edged by a scroll frame. It, too, has a torus enriched with a pattern resembling the one at the top.

The door astragal is found on the other side of the right leaf. Like the astragal of the door of Room 316 it has a modified Corinthian capital with a long, narrow fluted shaft and no base.

The lever handle is round with stopped fluting, ribbon, pearls, egg-and-dart, guilloche, and rosette. The plate is the same as the one on the inside of the door to the DeWitt Wallace Periodical Room, with two bands of scales framing a panel having crossed sprays of bay. The top and the bottom, in relief, are a cavetto with stopped fluting and rosettes.

On entering the Main Reading Room, we stand in a square chamber open overhead. Open means that this foyer has no ceiling of its own; instead, it shares that of the Reading Room 51 feet 1⅞ inches above the floor.

On this side, the flanks to the doorway and the door repeat that of the Catalog Room side; however, the two panels above the bars have fruit swags, fluttering ribbons, and a rosette, and pilasters replace the engaged columns.

The small antechamber is actually part of what is known as the Delivery Desk enclosure; it is a low compartment formed by two walls bisecting the Main Reading Room. It contains the book elevators, staff desks, and other equipment needed by those delivering

Cherubs over the doorway to the Main Reading Room.

The upper panel of the door to the Main Reading Room.

The lever handle and escutcheon plate of the door to the Main Reading Room.

books to readers, and also the Photograph Services. The doorway to the enclosure, on the west side of the foyer, repeats the design of the Catalog Room doorway—the same pediment, cornice, frieze, fluted pilasters, and astragal on the door leaf. The door is not as high, an element that permits an overdoor.

On the north and south sides of the room are doorways leading to the north and south halves of the Main Reading Room. They, too, are lower than that of the Catalog Room, because they must accommodate service walkways. On either side of the two doorways are barred windows. Between them and the doorway frames are beautiful high, rectangular panels framed by a cyma reversa with leaf-and-dart. The panel relief consists of arabesques made up of swirling acanthus, fruit cornucopia, fruit swags, flowers, and eagles. The lower parts are particularly fine, with urns topped by dolphins from which acanthuses spring. The base of the urn has the familiar device, rams' heads, seen in the bases of the lamp standards of the 42nd Street entrance as well as on the posts of the bronze railings on the Third Floor Landing. And there are lion paws.

Although the door leaves remain the same as the other two, they are sliding instead of being on hinges.

On entering the north half of the Reading Room and glancing back at the doorway, we can see how the architect repeated designs. The quarter engaged Doric column, the round pediment, and the broken entablature are the same as at the Catalog Room doorway, and the repetition extends to the embellishment.

The doorway is part of the north wall or screen of the Delivery Desk enclosure. It is balanced on the screen's west end by an exact duplicate, but there the door hangs on hinges. It is a lesson in repetition, so much a part of the classical tradition. When executed properly, as in the Library, it is successful, because it escapes the monotonous, an ever present threat.

We noticed the cherubs in the panels over the doors. Another cherub is to be seen in an upper panel to the right of the door. Here, he has a head and a pair of wings. The first one of these we saw was in the ceiling of the Gottesman Exhibition Hall.

Between the two doorways are eleven bays divided by twelve columns, half-engaged, of Roman Doric. Inside the bays are round-arched windows giving us a glimpse of the activity inside the Delivery Desk enclosure. A ledge runs beneath the columns and is supported by fluted consoles with volutes. At the top of the fluting are three rosettes and, above them, a tongue of acanthus, At the bottom is a modified lion paw. And, not to be overlooked, are Vitruvian scrolls directly beneath the ledge.

A volute support of the dado of the Delivery Desk wall. At the top there is an acanthus with three rosettes; in the middle are three flutes, and at the bottom is a lion paw. At the top is a horizontal strip with a foliated Vitruvian scroll.

OPPOSITE. One of the doorways in the north and south sides of the Delivery Desk walls. All four doorways are alike except that two have sliding doors and two have doors on hinges.

The columns support an entablature consisting of a frieze with panels divided by triglyphs bearing flutes stopped with rods and acanthus. Beneath each triglyph are three guttae, each consisting of a rosette in side-relief from which hangs a bell of acanthus. Between the triglyphs are panels with a scroll frame at the ends of which are dolphins, tails twisting, set vertically, with head down.

The enrichment of the cornice is modest, a band of acanthus leaf-and-dart, egg-and-acanthus, and leaf-and-dart. It is the parapet ornament that attracts the eye. It is a never-ending delight. At either end of the parapet is the horizontal volute at the side of the door frame. Between them is a alternating series of anthemia (palmettes) set on a fluted base with acanthus, a flaming urn on paired volutes held by a clasp of pearls and having acanthus, and a cartouche elaborately scrolled. One could point to the anthemion as being of Greek origin, the flaming urn of the Italian Renaissance, and the enriched cartouche as Baroque. Together, they equal American, classical, 1910.

Behind this parapet is a second one, equally low, with a modified guilloche where the large channels hold stopped fluting. In the center of the parapet is a clock surrounded by a bronze ring that has an inner circle of a cyma recta with acanthus-and-dart and an outer circle of pearls. The clock is modest compared to the wood frame that rises from the sumptuous front parapet. On its inside it has a circle of cable molding. At the top, interrupting the cable, is a pair of volutes bordering an acanthus. The volutes, transformed into acanthus, descend to a pair of broken cornices with dentil bands. Beneath the two cornices are two rosettes from which is suspended a splendid fruit garland.

The Main Reading Room now takes full command. It is impossible not to dwell on the great library interiors of the world, the *Prunk-saal* (magnificent hall) of the *Hofbibliothek* in the Hofburg in Vienna (on its shelves is the library of the great general, Prince Eugene of Savoy), the Rotunda of the Library of Congress, the Reading Room of the Bibliothèque Nationale in Paris (beloved of cast-iron experts and art historians), the one in the Detroit Public Library, or those again of the universities, such as Yale's Sterling Library, Columbia's Butler Library, the University of Illinois at Urbana, Harvard's Widener Library, the University of California at Berkeley. The Main Reading Room in the New York Public Library ranks with the Rotunda of the Library of Congress, but comparing them is like comparing Wall Street to Chicago's La Salle Street or the classical parts of Fifth Avenue to Chicago's Michigan Avenue. The two reading rooms are examples of wholly different treatment.

The clock of the Main Reading Room at the top of the Delivery Desk wall.

Dolphins to either side of a triglyph with stopped fluting on the frieze, and a Doric capital with necking above a fluted shaft.

The first impression is sheer size: the room is 78 feet wide and 297 feet long, the length of one and a half north-south sides of a Manhattan block. The height is 51 feet 1⅞ inches, that is, about ten feet below the height of a standard New York brownstone house. What makes the height so effective is that the ceiling is uninterrupted. By keeping the Delivery Desk enclosure low, the impact of the vast room is sustained.

It must be remembered that the great Reading Room, placed on the third floor, was an essential part of the Library plan drawn by John Shaw Billings. Carrère & Hastings designed the low-walled Delivery Desk enclosure to keep the room a visual unit. Only as the design evolved did Billings ask the architects to divide the room with a glass screen. This was strongly opposed by Carrère & Hastings for, to them, glass was, as it was to most designers of that generation, an *ignis fatuis,* a will-o'-the-wisp, a necessary but elusive building material. The architects in turn proposed a railing around the room three

A portion of the ceiling and the wall of the Main Reading Room.

feet from the book shelves. Billings had no use for this. The compromise came when both sides agreed to drop their demands.

The walls of the vast room are divided into nine bays on the west and the east. The narrow sides on the north and south have three bays each, which are treated much as the east-west bays of the Catalog Room. Inside the nine bays on the west are the large, round-arched windows, 17 feet 7 inches high and 14 feet 9 inches wide, in the upper half. The east side is limited to six open bays, with two blind bays serving to set off the ninth, or central, bay, also open, which is shared with the Catalog Room. We have seen the outside of the north three bays on the east side of the room from the stair landing above the second floor.

An entablature, which is the same as that of the Catalog Room, runs beneath the ceiling. A series of enriched moldings rises to a cornice adorned with voluted modillions bearing acanthus and with rosettes in coffers. A second cornice, forming part of the ceiling, is above it; this one has on its soffit a band of vine rinceaux with bunches of grapes. The ceiling's color of gold on dark brown contrasts with the imitation limestone of the wall.

OPPOSITE. A view of the Main Reading Room with its grand ceiling.

A non-figurative panel in the ceiling.

An oval cartouche in a scroll frame with winged cherub heads, acanthus, and a satyr mask with a collar of fruit.

The ceiling, as befitting the Library's greatest room, is the building's visual climax. We have been led ineluctably, as in the rooms and the stairs, from one ceiling to another, each different in its splendor; this is the most splendid of them all. It is divided into three large rectangular panels within which are large canvases of sky and clouds painted by James Wall Finn. Outside the rectangular panels are fields of abundant ornament. Two wide bands of coffers, filled with paterae in the form of rosettes, line the ceiling to the east and the west. Bands of vine and grape rinceaux are linked transversely between the large rectangles.

Each of the three large rectangular panels has its series of ornamental strips and sunken panels. In the four corner panels, which have an L shape, are oval cartouches in frames of scrolls and acanthus. At their top is a pair of winged cherub heads between which is

A scroll cartouche bordered by two winged cherubs and a satyr mask. Note the foliated Vitruvian scroll at the bottom.

a small bunch of flowers. At the bottom is a satyr mask with a collar of fruit hanging from his horns.

Between the two *L*s is a small rectangle, whose chief decoration is two arabesques springing from a winged cherub and two dolphins.

Off the four sides of the large inner rectangles are four oblong cartouches with figures first seen in the Catalog Room. At the top of each, what might be taken as a mask at first glance, are in reality three sprays of acanthus. At the bottom is a bearded satyr mask. To either side of each cartouche are winged cherubs with the scrolls of the frame above and below. Rinceaux circle outward from the cherubs.

The presence of the cherub, with or without wings, with a whole body or just the head, is very much a part of the Library's cornucopia of ornament. In fact, so popular was it in the first decades of this

century, as Pierce Rice has pointed out, that it took a special form in the kewpie or kewpie doll, the invention of the artist Rose O'Neill. That the cherub should be found in many places in the Library was simply part of the application of the classical, but there was the added incentive of its extraordinary vogue launched by Miss O'Neill and other artists of the day.

And the cherub is hardly the only figure on the ceiling. At the corners of the vast expanse are pairs of winged figures ending in acanthus leaves. Between each pair is a rectangle set in a scroll frame at the top of which are a bowl overflowing with fruit and, at the bottom, a satyr mask on scrolls and acanthus. Other pairs of winged female figures are found at the ends of the two long, narrow, stenciled panels running east-west between the big central rectangles. At the narrow ends are the figures, also ending in acanthus, which are somewhat plumper than their neighbors, and they lean to the realistic. Nearby, on the line of the long panels, we are offered yet other female figures rising from acanthus. With outstretched arms they hold aloft ribbon-like banners.

The overall impression of the color is simply dull gold on a dark ground. But the ground varies from tones of golden brown to brown to dark red to green.

The chandeliers are the same as those of the Catalog Room. The

Winged female figures, a vase of fruit, and a satyr mask adorn the frame of a rectangular panel.

Winged female figures, somewhat realistic in execution, support a rectangle from which spring rinceaux with cornucopia.

Acanthus in abundance on a Main Reading Room chandelier. Note the satyr masks at the second bulb row from the bottom.

bulb holders are in the form of rosettes, and the encircling arms of the lowest row have satyr masks.

The tables here, as might be expected, are thigh-high, with pedestals bearing the city's seal. The lamps are the beautiful ones of dark bronze with the sea-green shades. The chairs are of recent date, made in 1972; their design is simpler than that of the old ones and their color light instead of dark.

At several tables, there are small stands or lecterns to hold dictionaries and other reference books. The designers the Library were capable of bringing beauty to the humblest object. Here, the support of the book stand consists of a large scotia ending in volutes; on the long sides, the volutes are shaped like balusters. Four vertical beads divide the surface of the scotia.

The front of the stand also has its detail. There is a sunken panel bordered by a cyma reversa. To either side, at the ends, are sunken vertical panels, next to the top of which are double volutes encircling flowers. The whole rests on a platform with moldings.

The triumph of the room's furnishing is the bench in front of the electric indicator where readers watch for their call numbers and then obtain their books. Fourteen feet 4¾ inches long and 3 feet 1⅝ inches high, it is divided into two halves by a center arm and pedestal. The arm has an armrest curving into a volute and a rosette. From the

A reader's stand or lectern to be found at the end of several tables.

rosette, descending in a scotia curve, an acanthus comes to an animal head. The vertical back has, at its end, a sunken band of scales. Between the acanthus leaf and the sunken band is the center part of the city's coat of arms, four sails of a windmill separating two flour barrels and two beavers (the figures of the sailor and Indian are absent). The seal is wreathed in bay leaf and bayberry bound at the top by a fluttering ribbon. The seal is found on the inside as well as the outside of the arm.

At the top of the bench back are three pine cones set in cups of acanthus. The pedestal has, at its back, a continuation of the scale band. At the front is a volute with acanthus, the volute resting on a lion's paw. The pedestal has a base of Verde Antique marble, as does all the fixed furniture in the Library.

The floor in the room is of the familiar red Welsh quarry tile set in frames of Hauteville marble.

Inevitably we return to the Main Reading Room as a whole and to its ceiling. Structurally, the ceiling could not be simpler, consisting as it does only of plaster and wire mesh suspended from girders. The classical tradition freely makes use of the simplest instruments to attain its end. There is none of the nonsense of "truth" or "structural honesty," beloved of the Gothicizers of the last century, John Ruskin and Eugène-Emmanuel Viollet-le-Duc, and their followers in this century. If structure has to be concealed to achieve certain visual effects, the classical architect turns automatically to handy materials, in this instance wire mesh and plaster, and we glory in the result.

What is so magnificent here is that we have a vast hall uninterrupted by columns. Carrère and Hastings took advantage of the extensive surface to design a stupendous ceiling, which, for all its elaborate detail, is a single composition.

Great compartments mix with small and are bordered by coffers. The enrichment ranges from the Vitruvian scroll to the human form. All fits, all is balanced and proportional, all is joined by frames with decorated soffits. Equivalent examples range from the Henri II Room in the Palace of the Louvre to the Salle d'Hercule in the Farnese Palace, to the Basilica of St. John Lateran in Rome. America's great contribution to the galaxy of great flat ceilings is that of the Main Reading Room. And it is just one part of one of this country's marvels of architecture.

The bench in front of the Delivery Desk window where the reader awaits the books.

OPPOSITE. A view of the south half of the Main Reading Room, with the doorway to Room 315–S at the center.

XII

UNITED STATES HISTORY, LOCAL HISTORY, AND GENEALOGY DIVISION (Room 315–N) Room 315–S

ATTACHED TO THE NORTH AND SOUTH ENDS of the Main Reading Room are Room 315–N, where the United States History, Local History, and Genealogy Division is located, and Room 315–S, the Brooke Russell Astor Reading Room of the Rare Books and Manuscripts Division. We go to Room 315–N, to the north. The door, 10 feet 4½ inches high and 5 feet 10 inches wide, continues the seemingly endless display of classical ornament that is so much a part of the Library. Each leaf is divided into four compartments. The topmost has a relief consisting of a pair of rinceaux, whose upper ends terminate in flowers and lower ends, in heraldic birds. Between the two is an urn with strings of pearls. The second panel, a narrow rectangle, has only a rosette between two horizontal anthemia.

The third, or principal, panel, which is at eye level, is the richest. At the center is an oval cartouche rimmed by a string of pearls set against a scrollwork frame. At the top, part of the frame, is a satyr mask bearing a fruit-filled bowl. Rinceaux swirl from the mask. Beneath it, to either side, are birds. Beneath the scroll frame are griffons ending in rinceaux that curl into rosettes. The bottom panel, the fourth, is a rectangle, bordered by leaf-and-dart set on another elaborate scroll frame.

The lever handle and its plate were first seen at the door of the Main Reading Room opening from the Catalog Room (see Chapter XI, Main Reading Room).

OPPOSITE. *The door and a side panel of the entrances to the United States History, Local History, and Genealogy Division— Room 315–N and the Brooke Russell Astor Reading Room—Room 315–S.*

What is there to be said as our eye goes from the door to the ceiling and back again? In an age such as ours, wholly indifferent to ornament, we can only fall back to wide-eyed wonder.

Inside Room 315–N, the doorway has a frame of Rouge Jaspe marble. The cornice bears a shield. Above the cornice is a panel, an embellishment that comes as a surprise to even the knowledgeable devotee of the building. It depicts a pair of griffons with tails swirling into rinceaux. Between them is a vase surrounded by acanthus. The beasts face the vase; both rest a paw on its lip.

A central waist-high table has pedestals with little ornament except a diamond pattern. Inside the diamonds is the following cipher, *ALT,* which stands for Astor, Lenox, and Tilden. The style of the lettering is Art Nouveau, possibly the only example of it in the Library. The lettering is to be found on the pedestals of all the tables in this room.

The railings in this room are similar to those found in the Catalog and Main Reading Rooms. But instead of the posts' being treated as double balusters, they are square rods of wrought iron. Only the upper rail is of bronze.

The ceiling has a central skylight, covered over years ago. The ceiling is framed by a modillion band. Between the voluted modillions are coffers with rosettes. Around the ceiling edge is additional coffering with rosettes. These large coffers are framed by a Greek key band, a cyma reversa in acanthus, and a guilloche.

The upper part of the Rouge Jaspe doorway of Room 315–N. Griffons, a vase, and rinceaux fill the overdoor panel. Notice that the small shield directly over the doorway is held by a fluttering ribbon.

A pedestal of the waist-high table in Room 315–N. An example of the Art Nouveau style in the lettering.

Room 315–S is presently closed. Thanks to a donation of $2,500,000 by David Rockefeller, it is to be refurbished and given the name of the Brooke Russell Astor Reading Room of the Rare Books and Manuscripts Division. Still, it is worth going to it to see a panel to the right of its door. Similar panels exist on either side of the entrance to Room 315–N, but they are presently covered with plywood walls. We saw this panel first at the entrance to the Catalog Room.

The chief ornament in Room 315–S is a bronze relief set in marble. The inscription reads:

JAMES LENOX
A NATIVE AND RESIDENT OF THE CITY OF NEW YORK
BORN AUGUST 19 1800
DIED FEBRUARY 17 1880
THE NEW YORK PUBLIC LIBRARY
ASTOR LENOX AND TILDEN FOUNDATIONS
IN PERFORMANCE OF A GRATEFUL DUTY
HAVE CAUSED THIS TABLET TO BE PLACED
HERE AMONG THE BOOKS HE CHERISHED
AS A MEMORIAL OF HIS SERVICES
TO THE HISTORY OF AMERICA

To either side of the inscription can be seen a relief in bronze of a fantastic candelabrum. Here are vases with godroon bowls, dolphins heads, lion paws, acanthus, strings of pearls, and a flaming urn. At the bottom of the inscription is a band of ivy leaves and tendrils.

The marble doorway is a duplicate of the one in Room 315–N.

At each of the several divisions we can dwell on the extraordinary resources of the Library. The inscription in Room 315–S to James Lenox only emphasizes the fact. At the United States History, Local History, and Genealogy Division, the collections are a magnet for the American historian. So are the books and records for the genealogist, professional or amateur, tracking down family history. There are also the histories of cities, counties, and towns. For the New Yorker, there is precious documentation on the city, ranging from real estate and building brochures to an extensive photographic collection, including old postcards. If this division does not have a document the reader requests, the Print Collection, the Map Division or Manuscript and Archives will provide what is needed. Admittedly, Astor, Lenox and Tilden, the founding patrons laid the foundation of the Library, but with the establishment of the Library and the construction of the building, with the impetus of John Shaw Billings and his successors, the vast collections assumed the commanding presence they enjoy today.

A relief, in bronze, of a fantastic candelabrum forms part of the James Lenox Memorial in the Brooke Russell Astor Reading Room—Room 315–S.

uty to the Secretary of State Robert Lansing. With the Democratic candi-
date for the presidency John W. Davis in 1924, he formed the law firm of
Davis, Polk, Wardwell, Gardiner & Reed, today Davis, Polk & Wardwell.
He was president of the Library from 1932 to 1943.

The Trustees' Room is at hand.

The Trustees' Room.

XIV

THE TRUSTEES' ROOM (Room 206)

AT THE SOUTH END of the second floor, on the left, is the entrance to the Trustees' Room, Room 206 (visited with permission). There are two doors to this room. The outside one has the familiar "torch" lever handle, and the plates are the simple ones we have seen before. Those of the inside door are something different. Here, the plates are elaborate and stunning. Ribbons, pearls, acanthus, rosettes, and flowers in a vase combine to make them among the most beautiful objects in a building that can boast of its fair share of beauty. The treatment of the miniature vase and flowers reflects great skill, a common virtue of the crafts at the turn of the century. The handle on this door has a cartouche framed in pearls bearing the letters *PL*. It is encircled by leafy sprays, bound by a ribbon, that end in rosettes. From these rises the vase with two roses. The rest of the lever is a rosette in a small coffer and a boss in godroons.

Nor should the hinges be overlooked. They consist of bound reeds with a pinecone finial. Each door leaf has a sunken panel bordered by a ribbon molding. In the panel center is a circular bronze relief. The moldings consist of leaf-and-dart and curved acanthus rising at the center to an ovolo with leaf-and-berry around a rosette.

The overdoor, as is customary with Carrère & Hastings, is elaborate. Made of bronze, the rectangular frame has a cyma reversa in acanthus, a narrow band and bead-and-reel. Within it, bordered by swirling acanthus circling into rosettes is an oval frame made of a

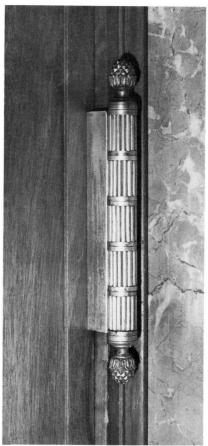

The PL lever handles and escutcheon plates at the Trustees' Room.

A hinge of the door at the Trustees' Room, with its pine cone finials.

Bronze rosette in the door leaf of the Trustees' Room.

As to fireplaces, Wharton and Codman say, "The fireplace was formerly always regarded as the chief feature of the room, and so treated in every well-thought-out scheme of decoration." So it is here. It has the most elaborate sculpture inside the building, the work of François M. L. Tonetti-Dozzi, who recarved two of the heads on the arches of the entrance portico. The marble is Eastman Cream from West Rutland, Vermont. The upper part has a panel with two supports, both maidens. The one on the left is holding a caliper in her right hand and has an oakleaf wreath with acorns in her left. The other maiden holds an hourglass. Between them is a winged scroll frame, topped by a grinning mask and supported by two serpents.

Two inscriptions are on the panels by the center of the chimneybreast. The upper one reads:

> THE CITY OF NEW YORK HAS ERECTED THIS
> BUILDING FOR THE FREE USE OF ALL THE PEOPLE
> MCMX

The lower one reads:

> I LOOK TO THE DIFFUSION OF LIGHT AND EDUCATION
> AS THE RESOURCE MOST TO BE RELIED ON FOR
> AMELIORATING THE CONDITION PROMOTING THE VIRTUE
> AND ADVANCING THE HAPPINESS OF MAN
>   THOMAS JEFFERSON

Below the chimneybreast, the mantelpiece has a frieze of rinceaux set between two shields. Beneath the left shield is the head of a young woman with flowing hair, wearing a helmet adorned with the head

FRANÇOIS M. L. TONETTI-DOZZI, sculptor, 1863–1920, was born in Paris and studied under Tony-Noel and Falguière. He assisted Frederick MacMonnies with the "Ship of State" at the World's Columbian Exposition of 1893 in Chicago and with the groups on the Soldiers and Sailors Monument in Brooklyn. He did the statue of Art in the rotunda of the Library of Congress in Washington, the statues of Venice and Spain on the attic of the old United States Custom House on Bowling Green, New York City, the sculpture for the Connecticut State Library in Hartford, and the sculpture for the garden of John D. Rockefeller in Pocantico Hills, New York.

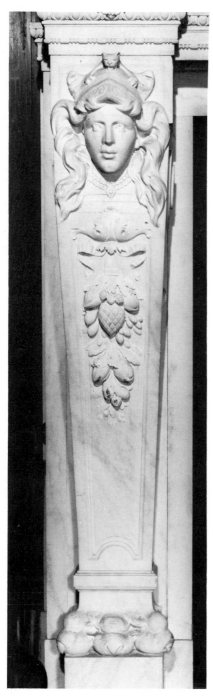

The head of Minerva.

The fireback and andirons in the fireplace of the Trustees' Room.

Minerva, symbol of intellectual strength, part of the fireplace in the Trustees' Room. Note the lioness on her helmet and the lion paws at the base of the gaine.

Profile of a satyr mask on the fireback in the fireplace of the Trustees' Room.

The mask on the andirons of the fireplace of the Trustees' Room.

The satyr mask on the bronze sconces in the Trustees' Room.

of a lioness. We may take her to be Minerva, symbol of intellectual strength. On the right is the head of a bearded Hercules with his lion-head cap; the god symbolizes physical strength. (Full figures of the same god and goddess, by Jules-Alexis Coutan, are to be found on the top of the facade of Grand Central Terminal.)

The cast-iron fireback matches the marble in detail. It has a sunburst, with the head of the sun-god at the center, which is set in an oval scroll frame, which is, in turn, set in a rectangular frame with crossettes and volutes. The volutes on either side bear profiles of satyr masks, reminding us of the satyr masks between the tops of the three doorways of the portico. The pair of andirons are in the High Venetian style. Gaines (half-figures in sheaths) are set on upturned obelisks resting on satyr masks. The right figure is that of a young woman holding a basket of fruit and, on the left, a bearded man.

The floor exposed in front of the fireplace reveals that it is parquetry, of Philippine teak.

The sconces are richly detailed in a shiny dark patina. Of French Regency inspiration, the central piece of ornament is a satyr mask with a full beard, pointed ears, and locks crowned in vine and grape. From the beard issues a cluster of acorn and oakleaf.

The large chandelier in the center of the ceiling echoes the sconces in patina and treatment. Along with a mascaron of a mythical being, we have here another version of the lion mask.

The ceiling is little noticed because much of it is in low relief.
Also, we must remind ourselves that it is best observed from a seated
position, and that this is the position of the trustees at their meetings.
The room, after all, was designed for them, and not for visitors who,
generally strain to look at what is overhead. The ceiling is a large
oval made up of a series of enriched moldings and bands. First,
beginning at the outside, comes a ribbon, then a cyma reversa with
acanthus, a Vitruvian scroll or wave, and an enriched leaf-and-dart
on a cyma recta with pearls.

On the interior, a wide band carries the relief, which consists of
figures set in a variety of frames with symbols of the arts and sciences
in between.

At the east end of the ceiling is an oval with the Athena Proma-
chos, Athena the Defender; at the west is Flora, with flowers and
fruit. On the long sides we find, on the north, a wide oval with the
figure of Science; on the south is the figure of Poetry. The frames
are made of pairs of dolphins. In four other, irregularly shaped frames

A detail of the ceiling of the Trustees' Room.

The figure of Science on the ceiling of the Trustees' Room and a female figure with a winged cherub in a frame of dolphins.

are cherubs at work. The frame to the right of Flora, for example, shows them as architect and sculptor. To the right of Athena, they are musicians, dancers, and a satyr cherub.

*An irregularly shaped panel in the ceiling of
the Trustees' Room. Cherubs are shown as
poets or writers. There is a satyr mask
beneath the frame.*

We can reflect again, as we have done more than once in the tour of the Library, on the role of the cherub or naked baby in decoration. We have seen the cherub as canephorus in the DeWitt Wallace Periodical Room. We have seen only its head, but a winged head, in the Gottesman Exhibition Hall. We have seen it in full figure in the ceilings of the Catalog Room and the Main Reading Room. Here there are more of them to be found than in all the other rooms together.

The importance of the baby figure in Western art cannot be emphasized enough. In no other artistic tradition does the human figure have so conspicuous a place. Of the various figures chosen by the artist and craftsman for its decorative value, the baby is far and away the favorite, a fact that explains its importance. In the Library it represents an added facet, namely the contribution of the sculptor, here unknown, in embellishing a great ceiling. What is more, the cherubs are classically executed in the great tradition ranging from the Ancients to Correggio to Clodion to the brothers Leyendecker in our own time. With good reason the artist Pierce Rice, as mentioned earlier, has pointed out that the baby is the very symbol of Western art.

The room has a centerpiece, a giant table with a top of teak veneer. It is 11 feet long and 4 feet 6 inches wide and stands 2 feet 6 inches high. The legs and stretchers are particularly elaborate. A pair of console tables stand against the marble panels of the east wall. The main support of each of these tables is an eagle standing on a ball, with a top of a half-circle of Black Gold Marble from Porto Venere, Italy. The black-painted oak chairs are of seventeenth-century inspiration, the more elaborate president's chair being inspired by one in Hardwick Hall, in Derbyshire, England. The chairs were made by S. Karpen & Brothers of Chicago on designs by the architects.

The four beautiful Flemish tapestries are new to the room, but they match perfectly the room's opulence. As can be seen from the titles woven at the top of each one, they represent the four continents: America is to the left of the fireplace and Asia is to the right, Africa is on the south wall and Europe on the west. They were woven in Brussels by G. Peemans between 1665 and 1707, based on cartoons by David Teniers III (1638–1685). They were given to the Library in 1968 by Oliver B. Jennings of the family associated with the Standard Oil Trust.

In each corner of the room is a bust: in the southwest corner is that of Alexander Hamilton by Giuseppe Cerocchi; in the southeast corner, Washington Irving, a marble copy attributed to Henry Kirke Brown after a plaster bust by Robert Ball Hughes; in the northeast

A ceiling panel consisting of the familiar devices of acanthus and a candelabrum base with lion paws.

A sidetable with eagle support in the Trustees' Room.

corner, Joseph Green Cogswell, the first librarian of the Astor Library, by E. Le Quesne; and in the northwest corner, by the entrance door, John Jacob Astor, unattributed.

It is most fitting that, at the close of this chapter, there should be a lagniappe for the illustrations. To this end, I have chosen a rare survivor among the special scrapbaskets designed by Carrère & Hastings for the Library. Typically, the architects left nothing to chance; the humblest object, a simple, useful piece of furniture, was to be adorned. One more lion head, with a ring in its mouth, and lion paws are added to the bestiary of the New York Public Library. In a sense, this scrapbasket symbolizes the largeness of spirit of the classical tradition that Carrère & Hastings brought to John Shaw Billings and his trustees. Nothing was too modest to be overlooked by the artist.

A Trustees' Room chair made by S. Karpen & Brothers of Chicago.

A scrapbasket designed by Carrère & Hastings for the Library, with the familiar design of the lion with a ring and the lion paws.

XV

THE SOUTH STAIRWAY TO ASTOR HALL

WE LEAVE THE TRUSTEES' ROOM to return to Astor Hall via the South Stairway. There is a repetition here as we find ourselves surrounded by the familiar. But what a joy it is to be once again in the hall where we were so splendidly welcomed on entering the building. The second portion of the South Stairway is twin to its neighbor to the north. Overhead is another barrel vault, and this time we are more conscious of its presence. Again, on the two sides of it are penetrations from four arches, the open ones overlooking Astor Hall and the blind ones giving shape to the wall on the left. The intriguing arches consist of the same sloped, stepped voussoirs. Where we have missed noticing it on the North Stairway we now see the band, with its panels framed by Greek key and rosette, which is carved in the bay wall inside the abutments and the arch.

The other curiosity is the use of the six guttae beneath the several broken entablatures, which are well modified. There is no architrave, the frieze is virtually nonexistent, and there are no triglyphs for which guttae are the customary fixture.

In one of the upper bays is the portrait of Samuel Jones Tilden by Daniel Huntington.

The view north across Astor Hall in no way loses its delight, although it remains unchanged since we last saw it, even from the opposite direction. It is such a reward to examine it once again and breathe in, as it were, its magnificence. Again, we can understand

OPPOSITE. A view north in Astor Hall.

why the candelabra are a perfect foil to the noble severity of the hall.

The same gratification is repeated at the landing as we stand beneath another of the stairway lanterns. Behind us, on the south wall, is an imposing niche for the bust of John Stewart Kennedy by Herbert Adams. Kennedy (1830–1909) was, like the father of James Lenox, a Scot. He first came to this country as the agent for an English iron company but he did not remain here until 1856. He joined M. K. Jesup & Company, later Jesup, Kennedy & Company, a railroad supply concern. Morris K. Jesup had a prime role in the nourishing of the American Museum of Natural History in its first decades. In 1868, Kennedy was on his own, working in banking. He was closely associated with James J. Hill and the Great Northern Railway and participated in the Canadian Pacific Railway. Active in Presbyterian philanthropies, he gave $1 million to the Presbyterian Hospital, now part of Columbia-Presbyterian Medical Center, and helped the Children's Aid Society and the Charity Organization Society. He built the United Charities Building, which still stands on Park Avenue South and 23rd Street. By no means, the least of his philanthropies was giving Emanuel Leutze's painting *Washington Crossing the Delaware* to the Metropolitan Museum of Art. When he died in 1909, he left an estate of $67 million, half of which went to charitable and educational institutions. It was as president of the Lenox Library that he was associated with the New York Public Library.

The niche is imposing. At the top is a giant anthemion, which fills a round broken pediment. The bay beneath is framed by two panels with reliefs that are models of their kind. Let us scan the ornaments on the panels from top to bottom. It begins with a flaming bowl resting on an acanthus-enriched base. Next is a pedestal that seems to sprout acanthus leaves. This is followed by another bowl, which is covered, and another pedestal, and a tall vase, with curved fluting. A covered urn is next and it rests on a base shaggy with acanthus, and then there is a plump urn decorated with strings of pearls. At the bottom is half of a four-sided base, the two sides in relief ending in hooves. Around the name and dates on the base of the bust is a mixture of rinceaux, rosettes, and, at the top center, an anthemion. The semidome of the niche has a large scallop shell, with the channeling partly filled with rods, flowers, and acanthus.

On the east wall is the bust of Thomas Hastings by Frederick MacMonnies. The plain bay and niche may best be defined as in the Greek Doric mode.

We can, at this point, stay in the building and go to the 42nd Street entrance and, there, continue the tour of the Library, or leave the

HERBERT ADAMS, sculptor, 1858–1945, born in West Concord, Vermont, studied sculpture in Boston and later in Paris under Mercié. He executed decorative sculpture for the Library of Congress and for the McMillan Fountain, both in Washington. He did the bronze doors of St. Bartholomew's Church and the Hoyt Memorial in the Judson Memorial Church on Washington Square, both in New York. In Brooklyn he did statues for the Brooklyn Museum and the Pratt Memorial Angel in the Baptist Emmanuel Church, also in Brooklyn. The Jonathan Edwards Memorial in Northampton, Massachusetts, is his, as is the statue of Chief Justice Marshall in Cleveland, Ohio.

building by the main entrance and proceed north, cross to the north side of 42nd Street, and stand across from this second entrance. The second choice is recommended.

As in Astor Hall, we can, once again, examine the Porch, Facade, and Terrace. And, no less important, is that the outside route to the 42nd Street Entrance permits a careful formal approach.

LEFT. The bust of John Stewart Kennedy, president of the Lenox Library, by Herbert Adams.

RIGHT. The bust of Thomas Hastings by Frederick MacMonnies.

XVI

THE 42ND STREET ENTRANCE THE JEWISH DIVISION (ROOM 80)

IN LOOKING AT the 42nd Street side of the Library we must do what we did on the Fifth Avenue side, namely, begin across the street. As might be expected, this facade has less ornament than the main one. But that fact did not limit Carrère & Hastings from achieving an equally monumental front. A terrace, an extension of the main one on the Fifth Avenue side, is to be found here, as is a short flight of steps leading directly to the entrance.

The façade has certain features of the main front. The base is the same, with its batter and rustication where the courses at the recesses are beveled. Above, the two stories are punctuated vertically by bays, which frame round-arched windows below and square-headed ones above. The keystone of the former, with its volute covered with imbrication and sprays of oak leaves, serves to carry the familiar lion mask with its ring, which is set against the sill of the window above.

To give emphasis to the entrance and to provide a central accent, the front at the entrance is advanced to frame a pair of Corinthian columns, which, in turn, frame the superimposed windows. This forepart or projecting part of the building is best termed by the French word, *avant-corps*. At the top of this avant-corps is the entablature, which circumscribes the roof line. Above the entablature, a pediment provides an additional accent to emphasize this entrance bay. The pediment, by the way, interrupts the roof balustrade.

Above, on the right, is the north wall of the Main Reading Room,

OPPOSITE. The 42nd Street Entrance Bay.

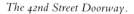
The 42nd Street Doorway.

rising above the building's main block. It, too, has an entablature, but here the supporting element of the cornice consists of modillions without the denticulated band.

The doorway is set in this avant-corps and bears a balustrade resting on massive ancones, or voluted brackets, carrying swags of fruit. The square-headed doorway has a keystone with stopped fluting and a frame of rosettes with leaf borders.

On coming to the entrance steps we can stop before one of two bronze announcements stands. Not only are they smaller than the ones on the avenue terrace, but they are also treated differently.

A bronze candelabrum at the 42nd Street Entrance.

To either side of the doorway is a magnificent candelabrum, lamp standards of bronze, modelled on ancient ones to be found in the Vatican Museum or, possibly, on Piranesi's version of the same as found in his *Opere* (vols. 11–12). The shaft consists of a series of superimposed acanthus crowns rising to a bowl with a fluted base. The bowl has a guilloche of alternating large and small circles on its upper side.

Perhaps the most fascinating portion of the candelabrum is its base, which rests on lion paws. Again the acanthus is present, but there are festoons of fruit bound with ribbon, whose ends each have a small weight, as well as bead-and-reel and Greek key. The climax of the base is the ram's head at each corner, with its chaplet of fruit garland and fluttering ribbon. The candelabra were cast by the Gorham Ornamental Bronze Company of Providence, Rhode Island, after a design by Carrère & Hastings.

Also designed by the architects are the bronze doors which differ from those at the Fifth Avenue entrance notably in having human figures. Of three panels into which each leaf is divided, the most interesting one is the in the middle. Here female figures rising from acanthus leaves support an elaborate vase with a scroll-frame cartouche. Part of the frame consists of a grotesque mask bearing the lamp of learning. In the cartouche are the letters PL. Note that the figures are executed with a distinct touch of realism rather than being straight classical.

A portion of the bronze door of the 42nd Street Entrance.

LEFT. *The bronze door of the 42nd Street Entrance.*

Just before the revolving door is a small space. Overhead is a splendid marble soffit consisting of a large patera in the form of a double rosette set in an octagonal frame of bound bay leaves and bayberries. On two sides of the octagon are rectangular panels of double guilloche, stunning examples of this beautiful device. Leaf-and-dart and an ovolo in egg-and-dart border the whole.

Before the installation of the revolving door there was a door with swinging leaves. Now only its bronze frame and overdoor remain. Scallop shell, acanthus, bay leaf, bead-and-reel, rinceaux, and leaf-and-dart enrich the bronze.

The bottom panel of the bronze door of the 42nd Street Entrance.

A panel of the triangular base of the candelabrum in the vestibule of the 42nd Street Entrance.

FAR LEFT. A bronze candelabrum in the vestibule of the 42nd Street Entrance.

LEFT. A possible inspiration for the bronze candelabrum to be seen in the 42nd Street Entrance of the Library. This one stands in the porch of the Villa Farnesina, Rome. Another is to be found in the Palace of the Conservators on the Capitoline, also in Rome.

We are now in the small vestibule with its rusticated walls of Danby/Dorset marble. Guarding the entrance to either side of the revolving door are columns of Roman Doric. Two small bronze candelabra stand at the point where the vestibule joins the corridor called the Conservators' Hall. The bases of both candelabra are triangular in shape, with sloping sides. On each of the three sides is a panel with a grotesque mask bearing a basket of fruit, while beside it are rinceaux ending in ram's heads. The shaft is enriched with arabesques, vases, lion masks, and beribboned garlands of fruit in relief. The top has a necking of fluting, sometimes called lamb's tongues, over a cable molding and, above the necking, is a godroon bowl, which curves into a band of egg-and-dart. The bronze bowl bears another of translucent stone with a Vitruvian wave.

It should be added that this bronze candelabrum has its source, in the matter of design, in a marble one to be seen in the Palace of the Conservators on the Capitoline in Rome or, possibly, in the porch of Villa Farnesina also in Rome.

The floor is paved with Grey Siena and Hauteville.

Once through the turnstile, we stand at a corridor leading to the Jewish Division, Room 84. Here is gathered a large collection of books and manuscripts in many languages on the Jewish people. The Division is noted for having one of the world's largest collections of Jewish newspapers and periodicals.

We are now in Conservators' Hall, whose main ornament consists of twelve Doric columns that duplicate the pair seen at the entrance. 11 feet 3 inches high they have monolithic shafts that are 4 feet 5 inches in diameter at the base. The capitals have an echinus in egg-and-dart and necking. All twelve are backed by pilasters, a visual echoing of the column. Above the columns is a denticulated entablature, as in the vestibule. It should be pointed out that the column shafts have vertical markings similar to those in the Gottesman Exhibition Hall.

On the west wall of the room are two plaques; the one on the right is modern and the one on the left is classical. The modern one reads, CONSERVATORS' HALL DEDICATED ON APRIL 14, 1982." Beneath is an inscription from William Wordsworth:

The rinceaux panels in Room 80 are made of cast iron, as are the modified Corinthian capitals.

> Enough, if something from
> Our hands have power
> To live and act,
> And serve the future . . .

The list of the Founding Conservators is to be found in Appendix V.

The classical plaque commemorates the construction of the building. At the top is the seal of the Library by Victor Brenner. Because it is of bronze, it offers a more sharply defined representation than does the white marble one of the plaque in Astor Hall dedicated to Brooke Astor. Here, again, we see a woman, sometimes referred to as Minerva, seated in a large chair with an owl on each chair arm. She clasps a book in her right hand. Forming part of an oval over her head is the inscription, NEW YORK PUBLIC LIBRARY, while at her feet, another reads ASTOR LENOX AND TILDEN FOUNDATIONS. To the left of the chair is a pile of books and to the right, the lamp of learning. Surrounding it all is an oval frame of bound reeds that are topped by an American eagle, which holds the city

VICTOR DAVID BRENNER, medalist, 1871–1924. Born in Shavil, Lithuania, near the Baltic Sea. Early on revealed talent for engraving. Came to New York in 1890, studied at the Cooper Union, went to Paris for three years and studied under Alexandre Charpentier and others. Most of his career was spent in New York. He is best known for designing the Lincoln penny in 1909, the obverse of which, with Lincoln's portrait, is still in use.

THE WEST FACADE. BRYANT PARK. SOUTH FACADE

IT IS ONLY NATURAL that, on leaving the wonderful building, we should feel that what remains to be seen outside is all anticlimax. But this coda actually adds a flourish to our tour. Partly it is learning how Carrère and Hastings treated the two remaining, lesser facades, partly it is responding to our curiosity to see what these facades have in store for us.

One device the architects had at hand was that of the terrace, which they carried around to the west front. Proceeding near the 42nd Street entrance, we can enjoy once again their admirable balustrade. They were supreme masters of the baluster. A more recent addition, sometime around 1960, is the low green wall, inside the balustrade, of *Euonymus kiauchovica,* a near evergreen shrub from China that the late Cornelius M. O'Shea introduced to Manhattan parks when he was borough horticulturist. It is far more satisfactory than privet, which was pervasive up to then, in that it keeps its leaves for much of the year.

At the west of the balustrade is a small structure of Milford granite, formerly a rest room and now a shelter for the carts of park food vendors. The handsome building, massive despite its size because of the granite, has modified cornice beneath which is a band of bucranes with swags of fruit interrupted by triglyphs with three guttae. Overhead, to either side of the round pediment, is a low parapet with a Greek meander and rosettes.

Carrère & Hastings evidently looked to the massive low structures around the Place de la Concorde in Paris, which today serve as bases for the statues representing the great cities of France. They, like the buildings on the famous square whose Corinthian Order served as guide to Carrère & Hastings, came from the drawing board of Ange-Jacques Gabriel. The oval window and garland were a favorite of the architect as they are also found in the entrance court of the Petit Trianon at Versailles.

LEFT. The small building near the entrance to Bryant Park on 42nd Street.

The entrance to Bryant Park is at hand. We go up the steps, turn left, and go up several more steps and then turn right to continue to a point near the Bryant Monument. Here we are in front of the rear facade, which has received more recognition from the architectural profession than from the public.

The chief feature of the marble wall is the row of twenty-eight vertical windows. The base of the wall is the same as that of the other facades, with its water table and battered rustication in Milford granite. From the rustication rises a flat surface of Danby/Dorset marble that is treated like a column with a base (the rustication), the flat surface (shaft) and, at the top, a very modified Doric capital and entablature. The frieze has garlands of imbricated bay leaves, bayberries, oak leaves, and acorns, the garlands suspended from and tied to rosettes of oak leaves and acorns by fluttering ribbons. These narrow windows are guarded at the bottom by grilles of halberds.

The principal element are the nine great west windows of the Main Reading Room which we have seen before in the north and south courts. They are stunning with their concave edges framed by rustication. Between them, just above the garlanded frieze are doorways with segmental pediments resting on ancones with guttae. Beneath the pediment is a square arch with a plain keystone.

At the top is the high entablature that runs around the building. Within the entablature, first comes the architrave with its three fascias set off by moldings enriched with pearls, leaf-and-dart, and bead-and-reel. A plain frieze is next. Last of all, at the top, there is the cornice resting on modillions, between which are coffers filled with rosettes.

The west facade of the Library.

Engraving of the base of the statues designed by Ange-Jacques Gabriel, to be found at the Place de la Concorde, Paris. From Pierre Patte, Monumens érigés en France à la gloire de Louis XV, précédés d'un tableau du progrés des arts et des sciences sous ce regne . . . par M. Patte . . . Paris: l'Auteur, 1765. *Courtesy of the Cooper-Hewitt Museum, The Smithsonian Institution's National Museum of Design. The book was in the library of Carrère & Hastings.*

207

The great windows of the Main Reading Room in the west facade.

A doorway with the segmental pediment and the frieze with rosettes, garlands, and fluttering ribbons.

The bronze statue of William Cullen Bryant by Herbert Adams.

In front of the western facade, in Bryant Park, the monument with the seated figure of William Cullen Bryant (1794–1878), the poet-publisher who did so much for New York City. In the generation before the Civil War he was the strong voice in *The Evening*

Post, calling for the great urban oasis of green that came to be Central Park. The bronze seated figure is by Herbert Adams.

As mentioned in the Introduction several members of the Century Association formed a committee to build a monument to Bryant shortly after his death. The coming of the Library made it possible, and it was dedicated in the autumn of 1911. Carrère & Hastings designed the setting, Neumann & Even, the firm that did so much of the modelling of the Library ornament, executed the modelling here.

The splendid statue is beneath a semidome with rosette, acanthus, bay leaf, guilloche and double guilloche, scroll frame, and urn (in relief) with a scallop shell at the top. Columns of Roman Doric support the arch in front of the semidome. Particularly fine is the pair of urns with bucranes, fluttering ribbon, and fruit swag. The bottom of the urn is gored and has cable molding, and the top has fluting and an acanthus boss. The urns stand on plinths adorned with scroll frames containing chaplets of pearls; sprays of oak extend from the frames.

An urn at the Bryant Monument.

We now can turn to the park itself. It is the finest classical public park in the country, surpassing Meridian Hill Park in Washington, D.C., and Grant Park in Chicago. Up until 1934, the grounds from Carrère & Hastings' terrace to Sixth Avenue (Avenue of the Americas) had been laid out in the picturesque manner, as evident from several pictures by Leon Kroll and other painters. Only a year or two earlier, the Architects' Emergency Committee, an organization founded to help unemployed architects, sponsored a competition for a new design. It was won by Lusby Simpson. He moved the Lowell Fountain, which had stood well inside the park, to its present site on Sixth Avenue and extended the Library's raised terrace around three sides of the park and put a large lawn in the center. The double balusters of the newer terraces were part of the scheme. Two other men on the staff of the Park Department, Harry J. Frees and Clarence Dale Badgeley, made suggestions for the details and the planting. The strips of flower beds in the lawn with Japanese holly borders were suggested by Gilmore D. Clarke. The original plan called for trimmed Silver Linden for the park trees, but in the end they were replaced by London Planes.

The Josephine Shaw Lowell Fountain, built in 1912, was designed by the architect Charles Adams Platt. There are also a statue of William E. Dodge by J.Q.A. Ward and a bust of the German poet Goethe by Karl Fischer. At the northwest corner is a statue of the Brazilian hero, José Bonifacio de Andrade de Silva by José Otavio Corraia Lima.

One horticultural curiosity to be found in the park seems to have gone unnoticed. In the ivy bed between the Bryant Monument and the Library's west front grows the hay-scented fern, *Dennstaedtia punctilobula*.

We turn again to the building. We must not neglect the wings that border the great facade. We can pause at the south end of the terrace to look at the avant-corps. As at the 42nd Street entrance, two floors are embraced by a pair of Corinthian columns. Other familiar decorative elements are introduced, such as the pediment and the keystone with its lion mask. The batter of the rusticated base is easily seen in silhouette.

As we step down to 40th Street and turn east, we pass the second of the former rest rooms, which remind us again of the statue bases of the Place de la Concorde.

The 40th Street facade, as might be expected for the service entrance side, is plain. Bays are set off by pilasters rather than by columns. Still, we know we are at the Library because of the presence of the lion head holding a ring in its mouth. Only the center bay has some differentiation. The lower window has concave chamfering. To either side of it are trophies hanging by ribbons; those on the left are made up of the instruments of the arts and the sciences, those on the right are weapons.

Above the roof, to the west, we can see a high chimney, a survival from the time when the Library had furnaces and boilers to supply its own heating.

A high granite wall runs along the sidewalk well in front of the building. The top course has a Vitruvian scroll. Two massive posts guard the service entrance. Treated as columns, they have a base with a torus and a plinth, a squared shaft in rustication, and a capital in the form of a modified entablature. The last-named has triglyphs with guttae, metopes with flat disks, and a cornice resting on plain modillions.

L'Envoi

OPPOSITE. *The south wing of the west front. The bust of the German poet Goethe is on the right.*

The tour is not over, nor will it be until we return to Fifth Avenue and stand once again in front of the great building. The sight of the familiar lions and the high portico calls up thoughts of the wonderful vistas and embellishments that gave us such pleasure. We cannot help but be grateful that the Library's construction occurred in the decades that produced our finest architecture, at a time when the nation led the world in the classical tradition. More, that there were giants such as John Shaw Billings, John Merven Carrère, and Thomas Hastings to plan and design the building and craftsmen such as John Lostis, Maurice Grieve, Henry Bonnard, and Michael Zawislan, only names to us, to bring their age-old skills to its adornment. Let us, their fortunate heirs, rejoice in their triumph, The New York Public Library.

The entrance bay of the 40th Street facade.

IDENTIFICATIONS, COMPARISON OF ORDERS, ILLUSTRATED GLOSSARY OF ARCHITECTURAL AND DECORATIVE TERMS, APPENDICES, FLOOR PLANS, INDEX

Pediment

Cornice

Pediment

Tympanum

Balustrade

Attic

Portico

Terrace

Vase   *Column*   *Bay*

IDENTIFICATIONS

Entablature

The Fifth Avenue Facade

Pediment

The head of the lampposts of the Library
Terrace

BELOW. The base and cornerstone

Finial with spike set in leaf cup

Raised fillets

Volute as pilaster capital
Modified egg-and-dart

Upright member treated as pilaster shaft
with panel of imbricated discs

Cable molding
Double volute with acanthus

Octagonal base in scotia

Echinus in modified egg-and-dart
Necking with rosettes
Astragal

Shaft with fluting

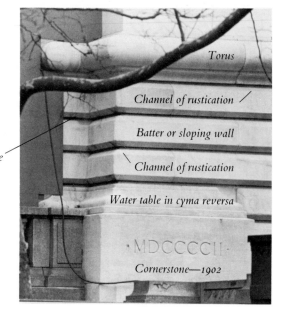

Torus

Channel of rustication

Batter or sloping wall

Channel of rustication

Water table in cyma reversa

Bevelled edge

·MDCCCCII·
Cornerstone—1902

One of the flagpole bases designed by Thomas Hastings for the Library Terrace

Beak molding
Fluttering ribbon
Rosette
Bucrane
Fruit garland
Modified egg-and-dart
Anthemion

Double volute in shape of seahorse
Guilloche filled with Zodiac signs

Beak molding in imbricated bayleaves

Cornucopia

Oriental mask

Swag

Cable

Turtle   *Anthemion*

The south fountain

Lion head with ring

Rusticated quoining
Double volutes with imbrication
and oak sprays

Semidome of niche with fruit garlands

Satyr mask with spout

Cornucopia covered with acanthus,
vine leaves, and grapes

Fruit
Scallop shell basin
Stalactite panels
Turtles

Double volutes with acanthus
and ribbon molding

Torus

Giant thumb molding

Cyma recta

The top of one of the doorways in the portico

Cyma recta with acanthus leaves

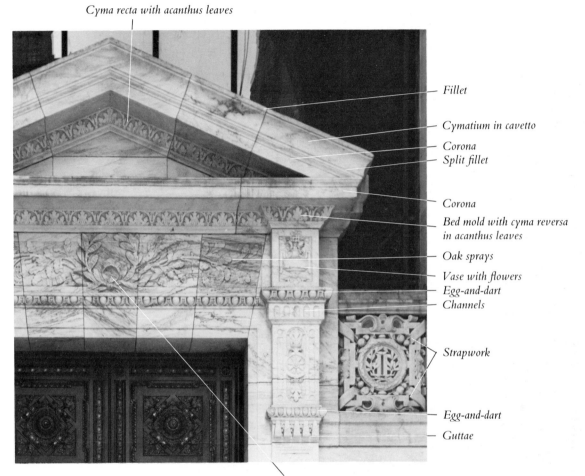

Fillet

Cymatium in cavetto

Corona

Split fillet

Corona

Bed mold with cyma reversa in acanthus leaves

Oak sprays

Vase with flowers

Egg-and-dart

Channels

Strapwork

Egg-and-dart

Guttae

Bayleaf wreath with ribbon

Panel with details of the bronze door

Foliated channeled guilloche with scroll palmettes (large circles) and rosettes (small circles)

Cyma recta with acanthus

Bayleaves, bayberries, acanthus, and fruit

Palmette in scroll frame

Boss with chaplets of modified leaf-and-dart, acanthus, and modified lamb's tongues

Channeled guilloche as above

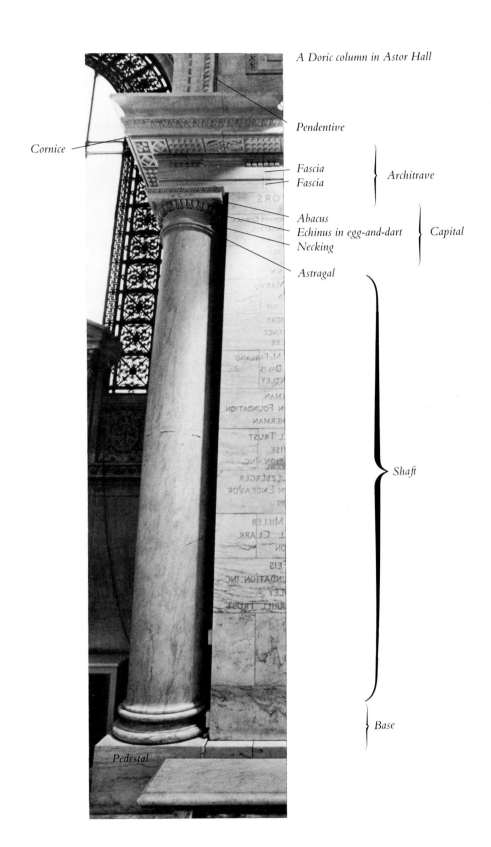

A Doric column in Astor Hall

Pendentive

Cornice

Fascia
Fascia
} *Architrave*

Abacus
Echinus in egg-and-dart
Necking
} *Capital*

Astragal

Shaft

Base

Pedestal

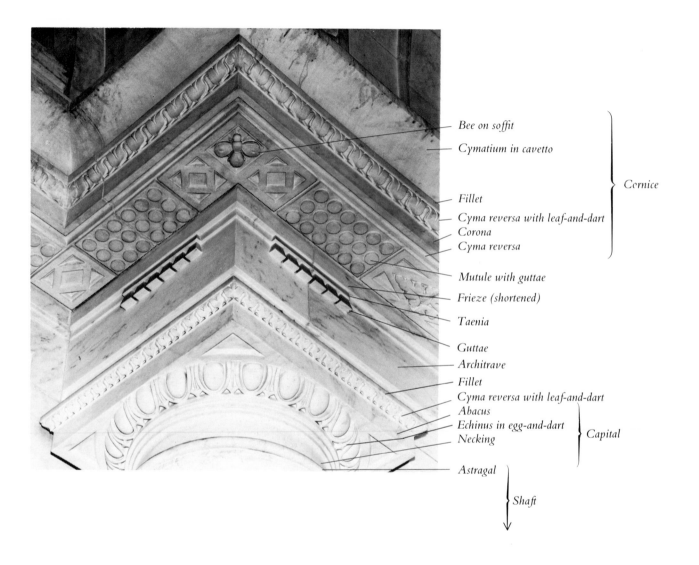

— *Bee on soffit*

— *Cymatium in cavetto*

— *Fillet*

— *Cyma reversa with leaf-and-dart*
— *Corona*
— *Cyma reversa*

— *Mutule with guttae*

— *Frieze (shortened)*

— *Taenia*

— *Guttae*

— *Architrave*

— *Fillet*
— *Cyma reversa with leaf-and-dart*
— *Abacus*
— *Echinus in egg-and-dart*
— *Necking*

— *Astragal*

Cornice

Capital

Shaft

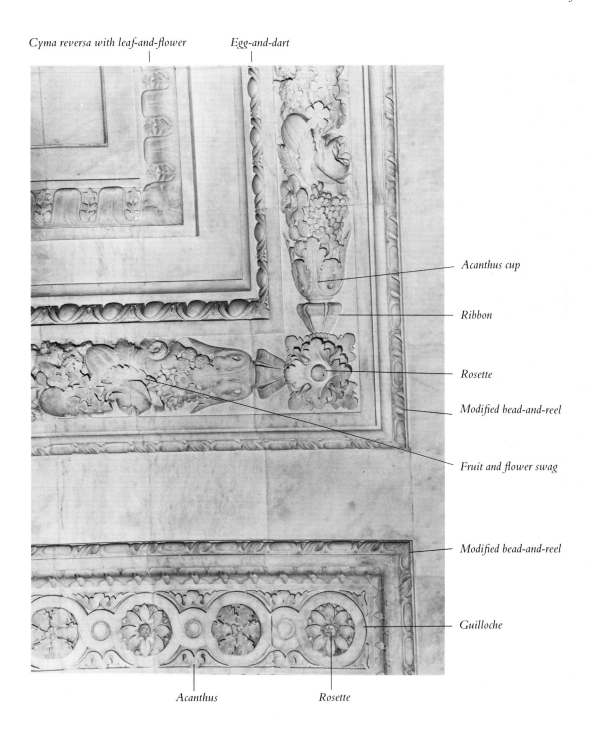

Cyma reversa with leaf-and-flower

Egg-and-dart

Acanthus cup

Ribbon

Rosette

Modified bead-and-reel

Fruit and flower swag

Modified bead-and-reel

Guilloche

Acanthus

Rosette

One of the candelabra in Astor Hall

Bronze arms with lion heads and acanthus

Modified egg-and-dart on cavetto
Underside scotia with acanthus
Gored bowl
Torus in cable molding
Necking

Torus in cable molding

Sleeve

Belly

Scotia in acanthus

Large cyma reversa with acanthus

Torus with ribbon and acanthus

Large acanthus

*Base with bucrane, ribbon, husk strands,
and ox hooves*

Plinth

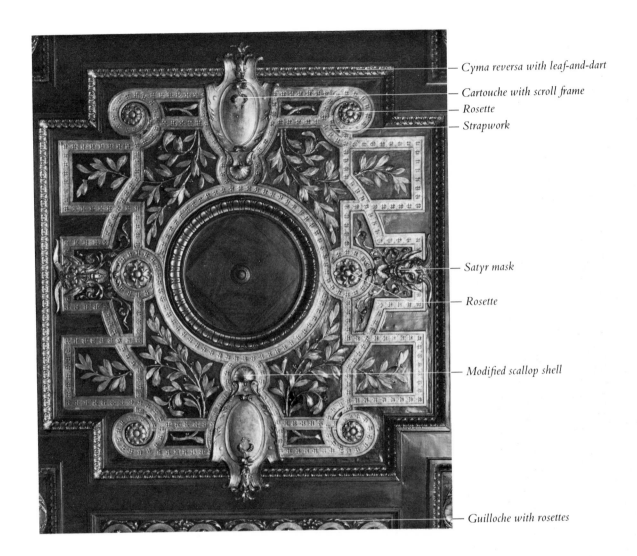

A flat panel of stucco relief at the center
Ceiling panel South-North Gallery

— *Cyma reversa with leaf-and-dart*

— *Cartouche with scroll frame*
— *Rosette*
— *Strapwork*

— *Satyr mask*

— *Rosette*

— *Modified scallop shell*

— *Guilloche with rosettes*

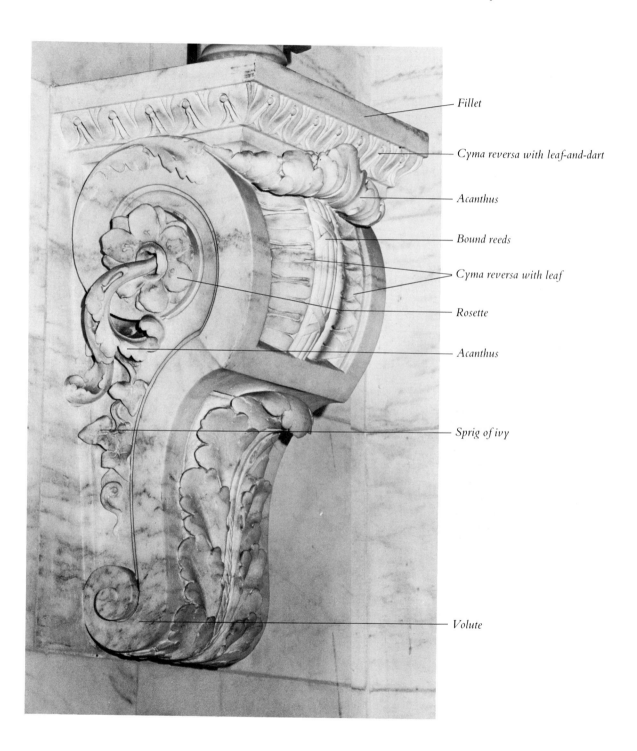

A giant bracket in the South–North Gallery

— Fillet

— *Cyma reversa with leaf-and-dart*

— *Acanthus*

— *Bound reeds*

— *Cyma reversa with leaf*

— *Rosette*

— *Acanthus*

— *Sprig of ivy*

— *Volute*

Raking cornice

Ovolo with egg-and-dart

Fillet   Cymatium in cavetto   Corona

The pediment on the inside of the Exhibition Hall doorway

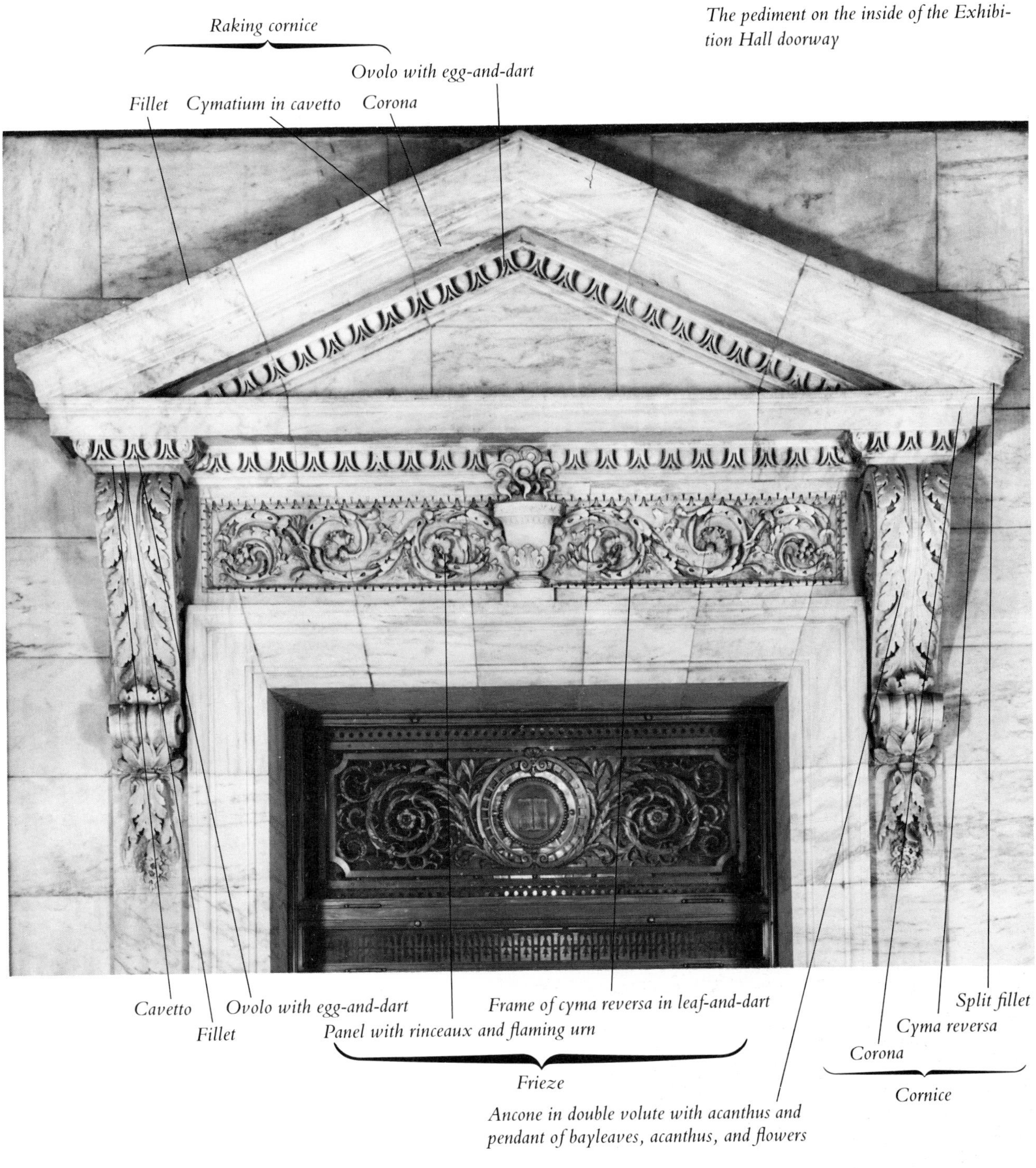

Cavetto
Fillet
Ovolo with egg-and-dart
Panel with rinceaux and flaming urn

Frame of cyma reversa in leaf-and-dart

Split fillet
Cyma reversa
Corona
Cornice

Frieze

Ancone in double volute with acanthus and pendant of bayleaves, acanthus, and flowers

The top of the Doric column in the Exhibition Hall

— *Cavetto with acanthus*
— *Bead-and-reel*

— *Frieze with rinceaux*

— *Fillet* ⎫
⎬ *Abacus*
— *Cyma reversa* ⎭
— *Echinus with egg-and-dart*
— *Soffit panel with Greek key and sprig of bay*

— *Volute with rosette*

— *Bead-and-reel*

— *Shaft*

— *Fruit pendant hanging from acanthus*

— *Satyr mask in scroll frame*

— *Scrolls with acanthus*

— *Arabesque of plants*
— *Cabuchon in scroll frame*

— *Anthemia and flowers
between flowing ribbon*

— *Scrolls*

— *Guilloche*
— *Fruit garland*

Satyr mask with bowl of fruit on head

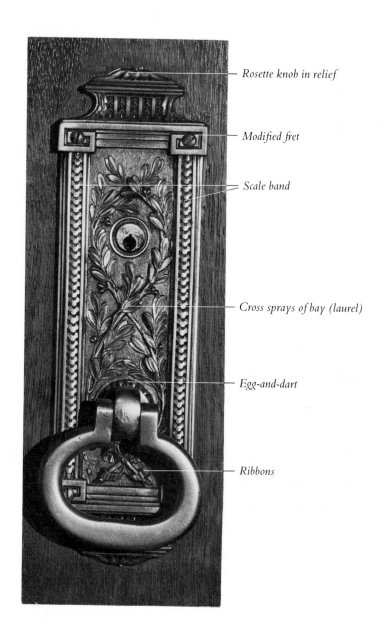

Drop Ring and plate at the DeWitt
Wallace Periodical Room

Rosette knob in relief

Modified fret

Scale band

Cross sprays of bay (laurel)

Egg-and-dart

Ribbons

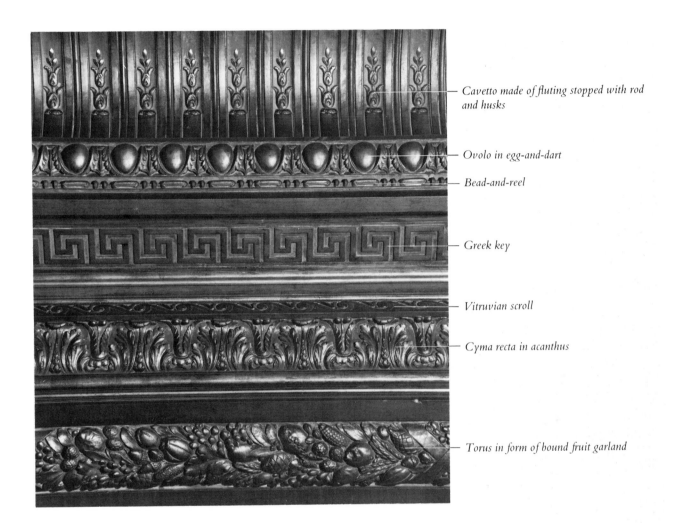

Part of the ceiling enrichment in the Periodical Room

— Cavetto made of fluting stopped with rod and husks

— Ovolo in egg-and-dart

— Bead-and-reel

— Greek key

— Vitruvian scroll

— Cyma recta in acanthus

— Torus in form of bound fruit garland

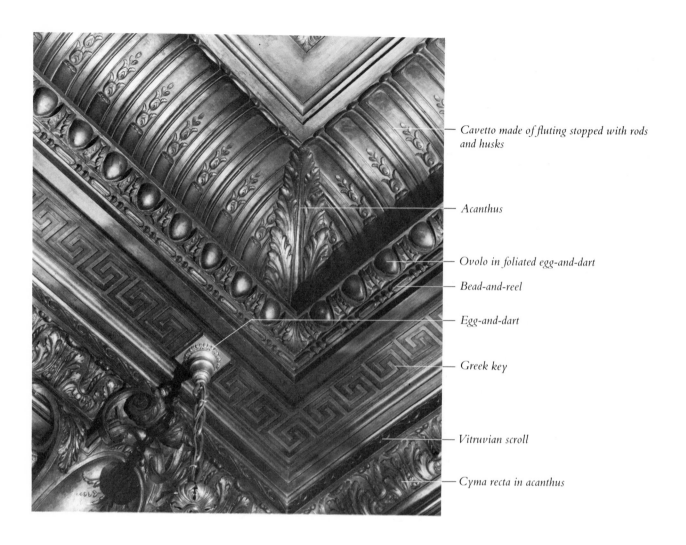

*Part of the ceiling and chandelier enrichment
in the Periodical Room*

— *Cavetto made of fluting stopped with rods
and husks*

— *Acanthus*

— *Ovolo in foliated egg-and-dart*

— *Bead-and-reel*

— *Egg-and-dart*

— *Greek key*

— *Vitruvian scroll*

— *Cyma recta in acanthus*

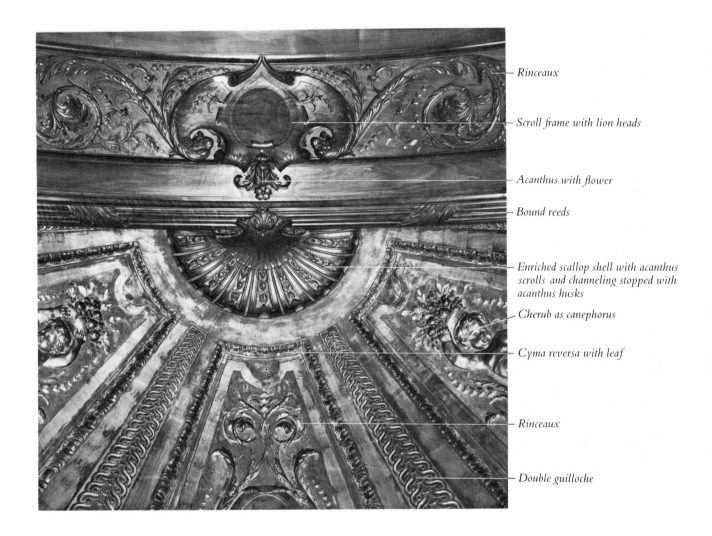

Rinceaux

Scroll frame with lion heads

Acanthus with flower

Bound reeds

Enriched scallop shell with acanthus scrolls and channeling stopped with acanthus husks

Cherub as canephorus

Cyma reversa with leaf

Rinceaux

Double guilloche

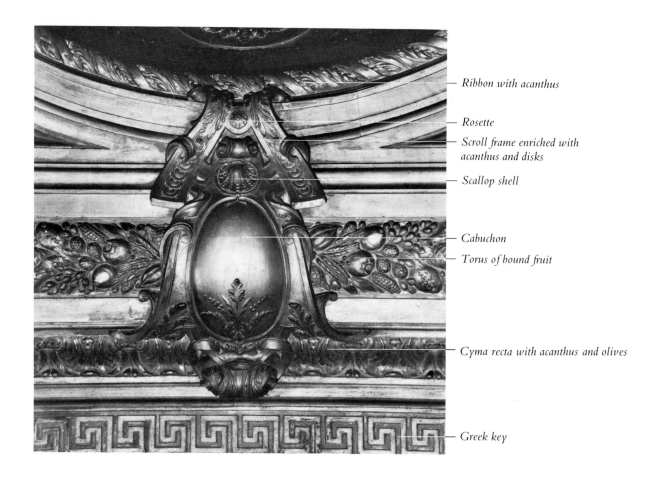

A cartouche, a Renaissance device, on the ceiling of the Periodical Room

Ribbon with acanthus

Rosette

Scroll frame enriched with acanthus and disks

Scallop shell

Cabuchon

Torus of bound fruit

Cyma recta with acanthus and olives

Greek key

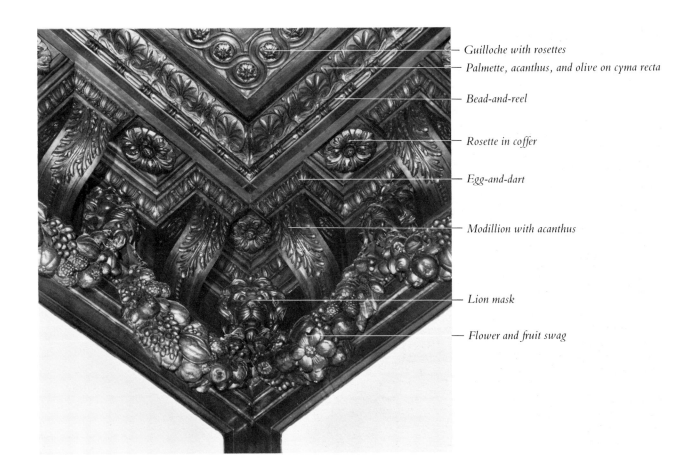

A corner of the cornice and ceiling of the Periodical Room

— Guilloche with rosettes

— Palmette, acanthus, and olive on cyma recta

— Bead-and-reel

— Rosette in coffer

— Egg-and-dart

— Modillion with acanthus

— Lion mask

— Flower and fruit swag

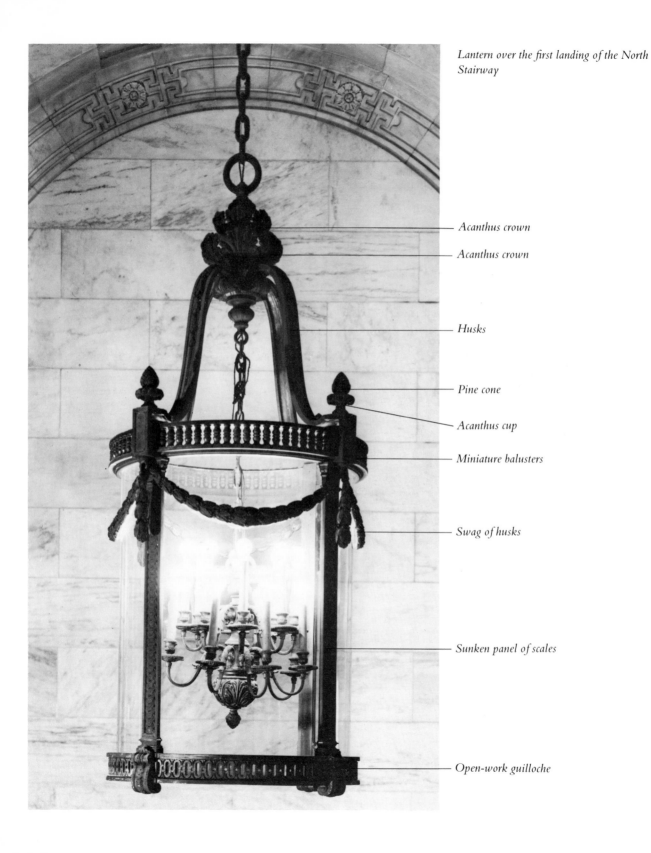

Lantern over the first landing of the North Stairway

— *Acanthus crown*

— *Acanthus crown*

— *Husks*

— *Pine cone*

— *Acanthus cup*

— *Miniature balusters*

— *Swag of husks*

— *Sunken panel of scales*

— *Open-work guilloche*

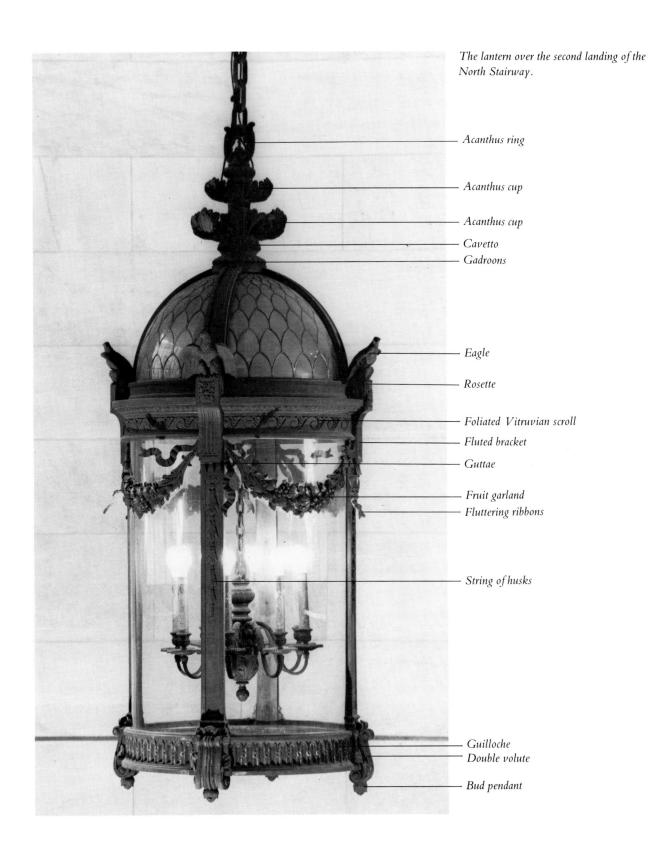

The lantern over the second landing of the North Stairway.

— *Acanthus ring*

— *Acanthus cup*

— *Acanthus cup*

— *Cavetto*
— *Gadroons*

— *Eagle*

— *Rosette*

— *Foliated Vitruvian scroll*

— *Fluted bracket*

— *Guttae*

— *Fruit garland*
— *Fluttering ribbons*

— *String of husks*

— *Guilloche*
— *Double volute*

— *Bud pendant*

Sloping splayed voussoirs

Rosette in square coffer

Cyma reversa with leaf-and-dart

Rosette in octagonal coffer

Egg-and-dart

Cyma reversa in leaf-and-dart

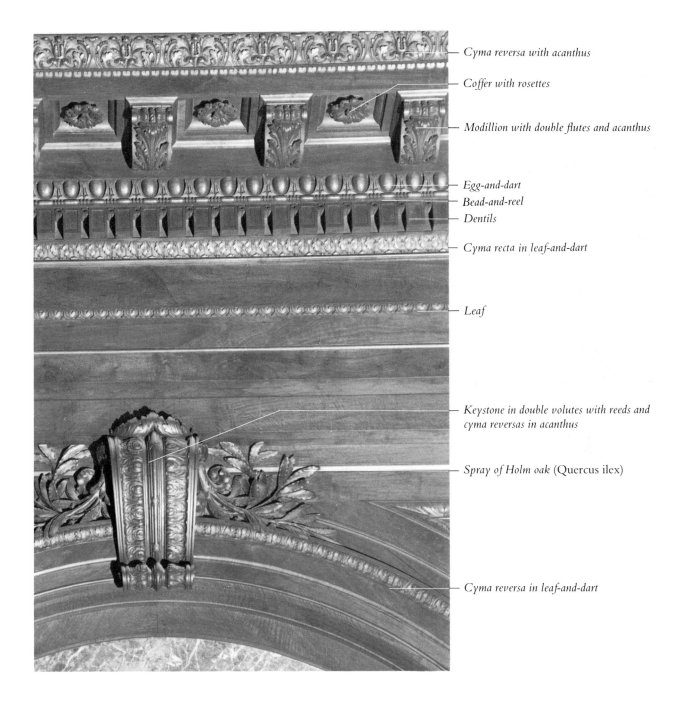

The top of an arch and the modified enta-
blature in the Third Floor Landing Hall

— *Cyma reversa with acanthus*

— *Coffer with rosettes*

— *Modillion with double flutes and acanthus*

— *Egg-and-dart*
— *Bead-and-reel*
— *Dentils*
— *Cyma recta in leaf-and-dart*

— *Leaf*

— *Keystone in double volutes with reeds and*
cyma reversas in acanthus

— *Spray of Holm oak (Quercus ilex)*

— *Cyma reversa in leaf-and-dart*

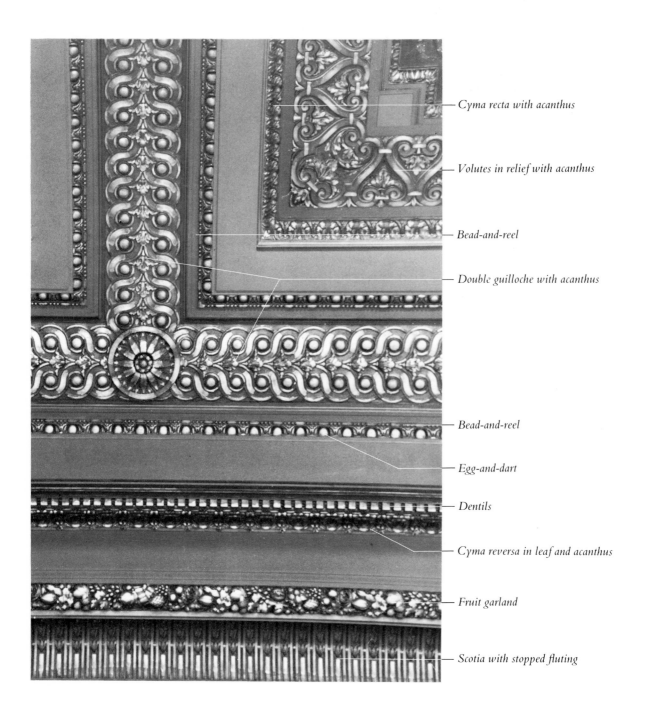

— Cyma recta with acanthus

— Volutes in relief with acanthus

— Bead-and-reel

— Double guilloche with acanthus

— Bead-and-reel

— Egg-and-dart

— Dentils

— Cyma reversa in leaf and acanthus

— Fruit garland

— Scotia with stopped fluting

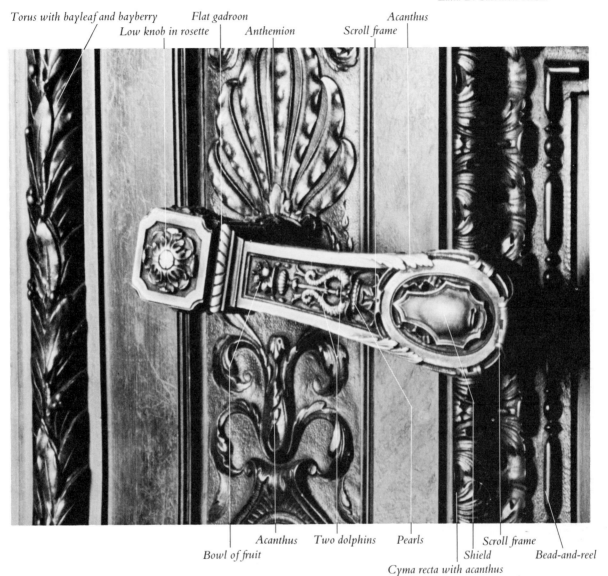

The Dolphin lever handle of the door to the
Edna B. Salomon Room

Torus with bayleaf and bayberry   Flat gadroon   Acanthus
      Low knob in rosette   Anthemion   Scroll frame

Acanthus   Two dolphins   Pearls   Scroll frame
Bowl of fruit   Shield   Bead-and-reel
                      Cyma recta with acanthus

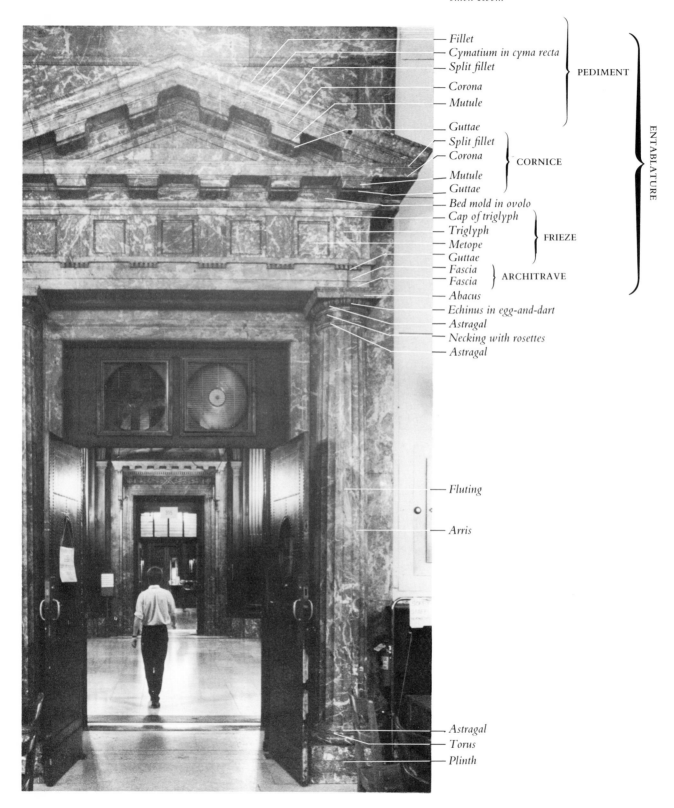

The Doric doorway inside the Edna B. Salomon Room

— Fillet
— Cymatium in cyma recta
— Split fillet
— Corona
— Mutule

PEDIMENT

— Guttae
— Split fillet
— Corona
— Mutule
— Guttae

CORNICE

— Bed mold in ovolo
— Cap of triglyph
— Triglyph
— Metope
— Guttae

FRIEZE

— Fascia
— Fascia

ARCHITRAVE

— Abacus
— Echinus in egg-and-dart
— Astragal
— Necking with rosettes
— Astragal

ENTABLATURE

— Fluting

— Arris

— Astragal
— Torus
— Plinth

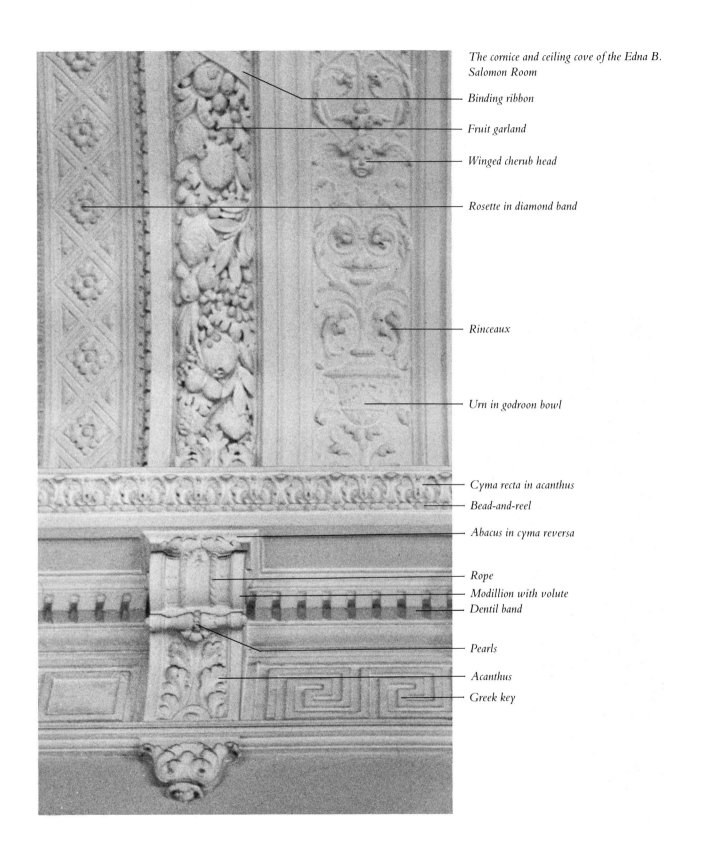

The cornice and ceiling cove of the Edna B. Salomon Room

— Binding ribbon

— Fruit garland

— Winged cherub head

— Rosette in diamond band

— Rinceaux

— Urn in godroon bowl

— Cyma recta in acanthus

— Bead-and-reel

— Abacus in cyma reversa

— Rope

— Modillion with volute

— Dentil band

— Pearls

— Acanthus

— Greek key

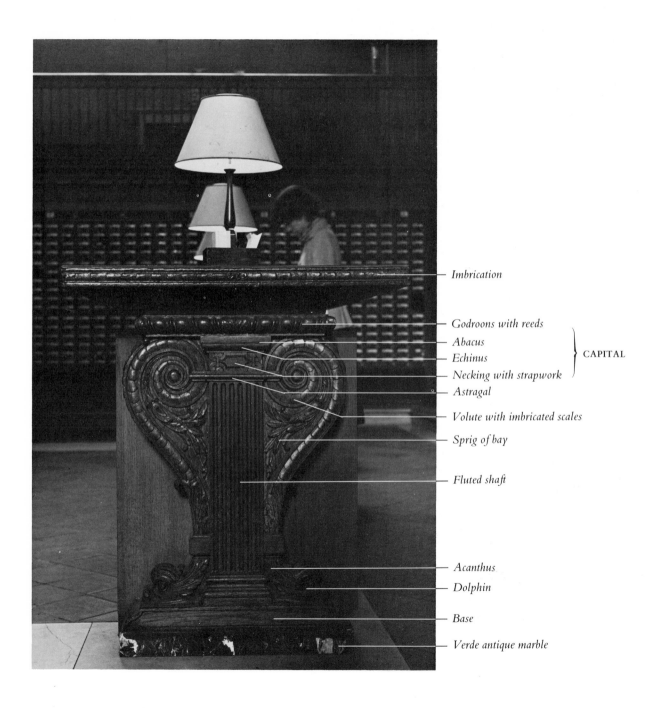

A pedestal of the waist-high table in the Catalog Room

— Imbrication

— Godroons with reeds
— Abacus
— Echinus   } CAPITAL
— Necking with strapwork
— Astragal

— Volute with imbricated scales

— Sprig of bay

— Fluted shaft

— Acanthus
— Dolphin

— Base

— Verde antique marble

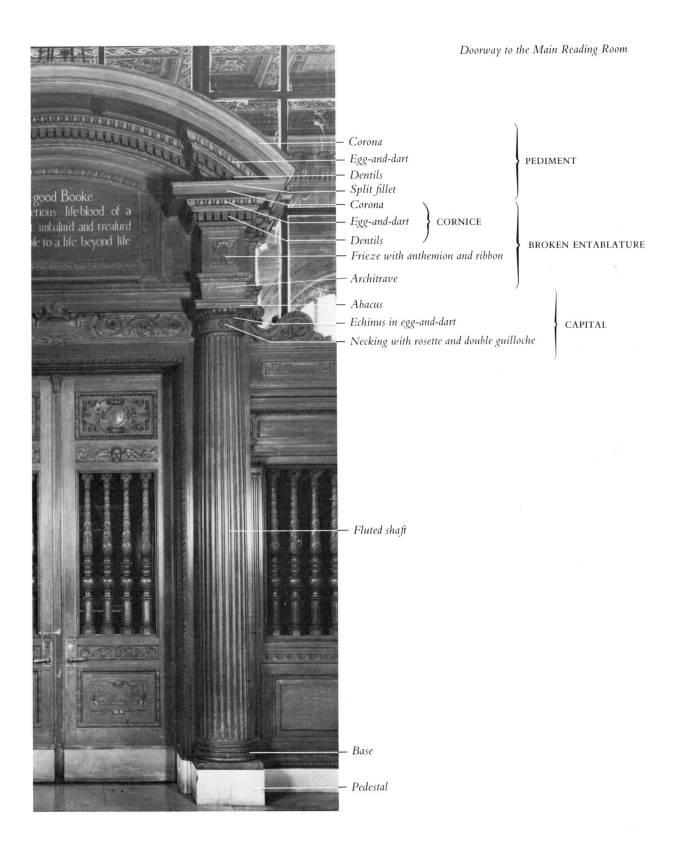

— Corona
— Egg-and-dart   } PEDIMENT
— Dentils
— Split fillet
— Corona
— Egg-and-dart   } CORNICE
— Dentils   } BROKEN ENTABLATURE
— Frieze with anthemion and ribbon
— Architrave
— Abacus
— Echinus in egg-and-dart   } CAPITAL
— Necking with rosette and double guilloche

good Booke
etious life-blood of a
, imbalm'd and treafurd
fe to a life beyond life

— Fluted shaft

— Base

— Pedestal

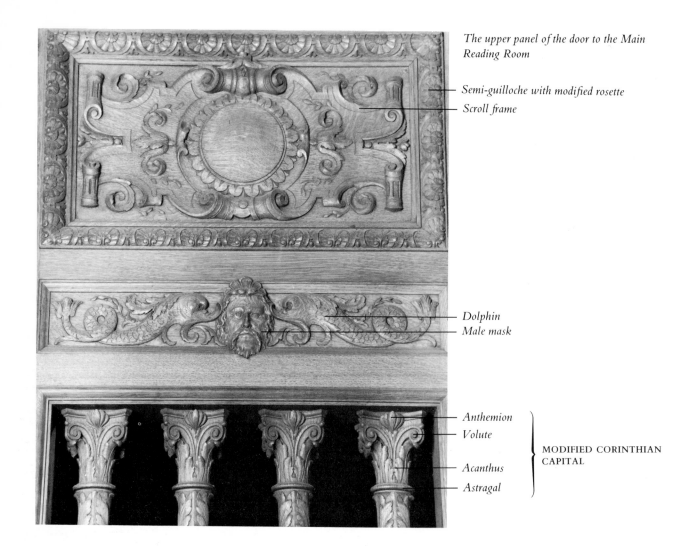

The upper panel of the door to the Main Reading Room

Semi-guilloche with modified rosette
Scroll frame

Dolphin
Male mask

Anthemion
Volute

MODIFIED CORINTHIAN
CAPITAL

Acanthus
Astragal

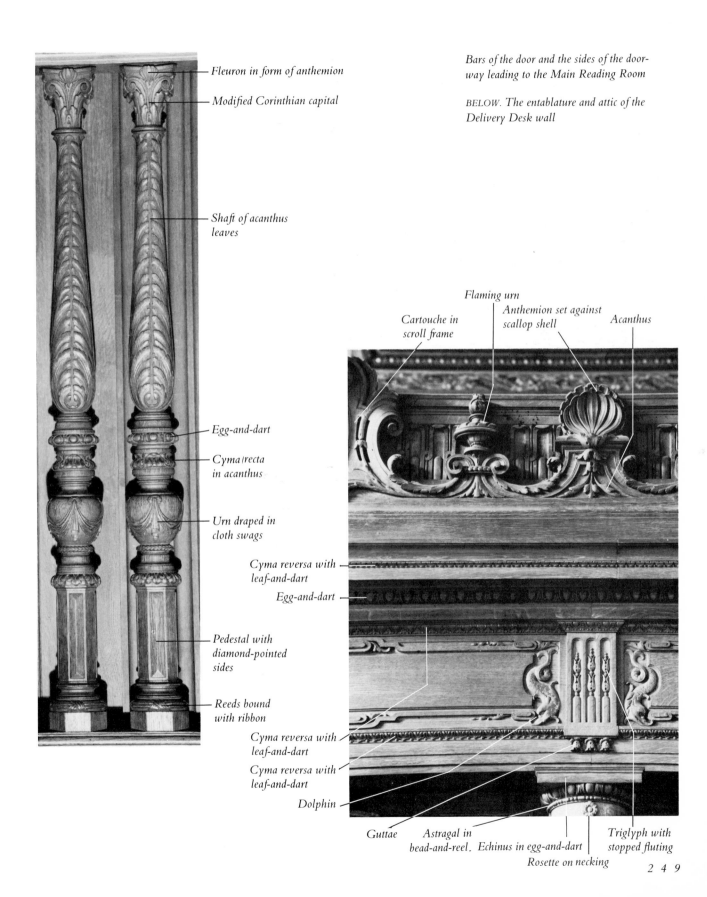

Fleuron in form of anthemion

Modified Corinthian capital

Shaft of acanthus leaves

Egg-and-dart

Cyma recta in acanthus

Urn draped in cloth swags

Pedestal with diamond-pointed sides

Reeds bound with ribbon

Cyma reversa with leaf-and-dart

Cyma reversa with leaf-and-dart

Dolphin

Bars of the door and the sides of the doorway leading to the Main Reading Room

BELOW. The entablature and attic of the Delivery Desk wall

Cartouche in scroll frame

Flaming urn

Anthemion set against scallop shell

Acanthus

Cyma reversa with leaf-and-dart

Egg-and-dart

Guttae   Astragal in bead-and-reel.   Echinus in egg-and-dart

Rosette on necking

Triglyph with stopped fluting

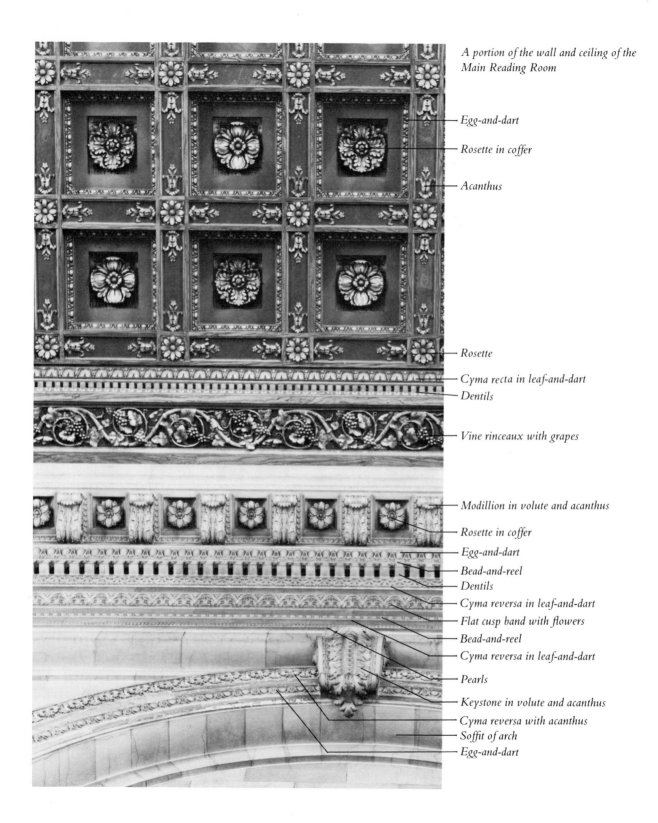

A portion of the wall and ceiling of the Main Reading Room

Egg-and-dart

Rosette in coffer

Acanthus

Rosette

Cyma recta in leaf-and-dart

Dentils

Vine rinceaux with grapes

Modillion in volute and acanthus

Rosette in coffer

Egg-and-dart

Bead-and-reel

Dentils

Cyma reversa in leaf-and-dart

Flat cusp band with flowers

Bead-and-reel

Cyma reversa in leaf-and-dart

Pearls

Keystone in volute and acanthus

Cyma reversa with acanthus

Soffit of arch

Egg-and-dart

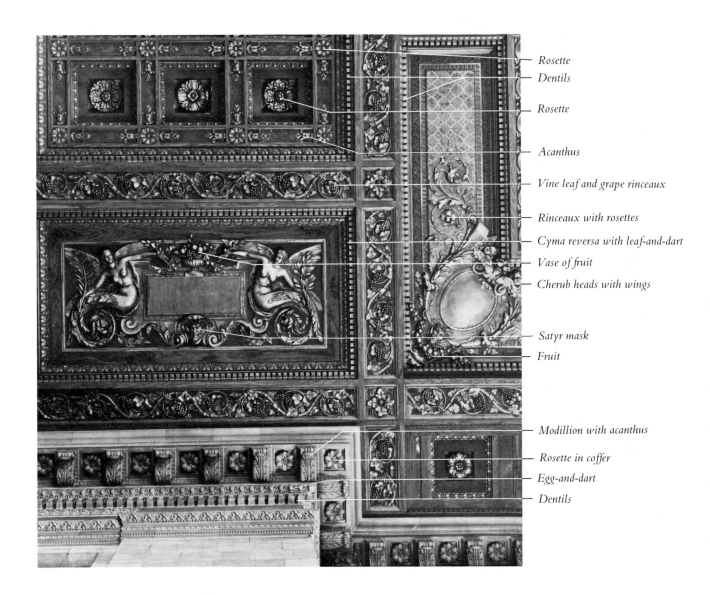

A portion of the ceiling of the Main Reading Room

— Rosette
— Dentils

— Rosette

— Acanthus

— Vine leaf and grape rinceaux

— Rinceaux with rosettes
— Cyma reversa with leaf-and-dart
— Vase of fruit
— Cherub heads with wings

— Satyr mask
— Fruit

— Modillion with acanthus

— Rosette in coffer

— Egg-and-dart

— Dentils

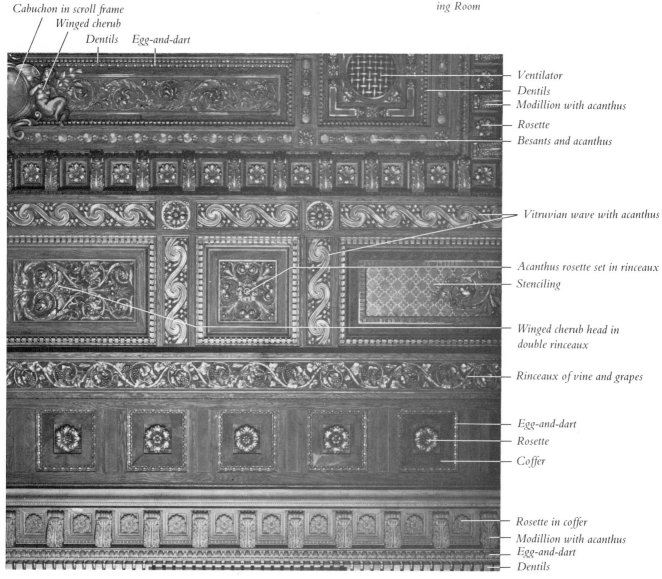

A portion of the ceiling of the Main Reading Room

Cabuchon in scroll frame
Winged cherub
Dentils   Egg-and-dart

Ventilator
Dentils
Modillion with acanthus
Rosette
Besants and acanthus

Vitruvian wave with acanthus

Acanthus rosette set in rinceaux
Stenciling

Winged cherub head in double rinceaux

Rinceaux of vine and grapes

Egg-and-dart
Rosette
Coffer

Rosette in coffer
Modillion with acanthus
Egg-and-dart
Dentils

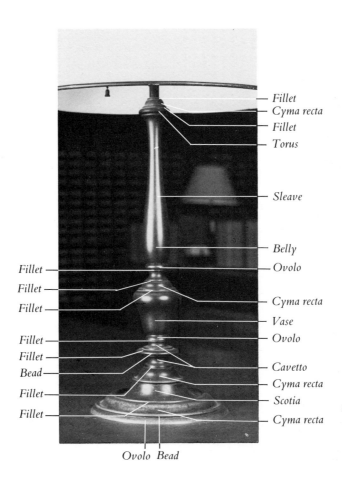

Fillet
Cyma recta
Fillet
Torus

Sleave

Belly
Ovolo

Fillet
Fillet
Fillet

Cyma recta
Vase
Ovolo

Fillet
Fillet
Bead

Cavetto
Cyma recta
Scotia

Fillet
Fillet

Cyma recta

Ovolo Bead

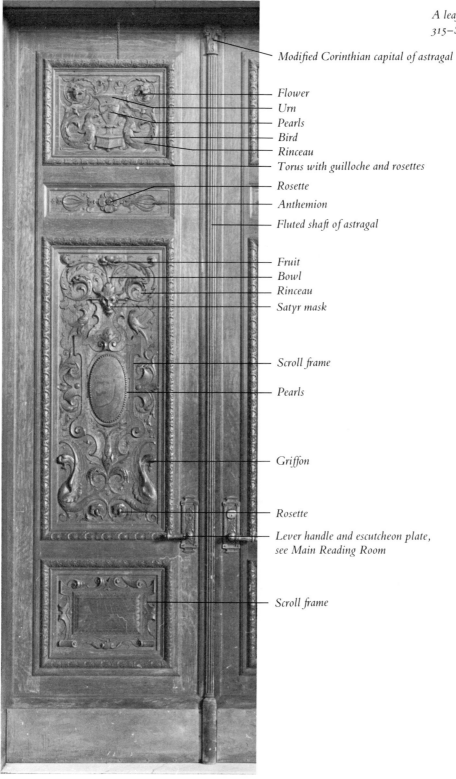

Modified Corinthian capital of astragal

Flower
Urn
Pearls
Bird
Rinceau
Torus with guilloche and rosettes

Rosette
Anthemion

Fluted shaft of astragal

Fruit
Bowl
Rinceau
Satyr mask

Scroll frame

Pearls

Griffon

Rosette

Lever handle and escutcheon plate, see Main Reading Room

Scroll frame

A panel to the sides of the doorways to Rooms 315–N and 315–S. The same panels are also to be found on the inside of the doorway in the Catalog Room going to the Third Floor Landing

Egg-and-dart
Necking

Ear of wheat
Fluting
Fillet
Rinceau

Cyma reversa with leaf-and-dart
Anthemion

Scroll frame
Pearls

Cartouche with a lily of acanthus leaves

Basket of fruit

Fruit garland
Winged sphinx as canephorus

Rosette

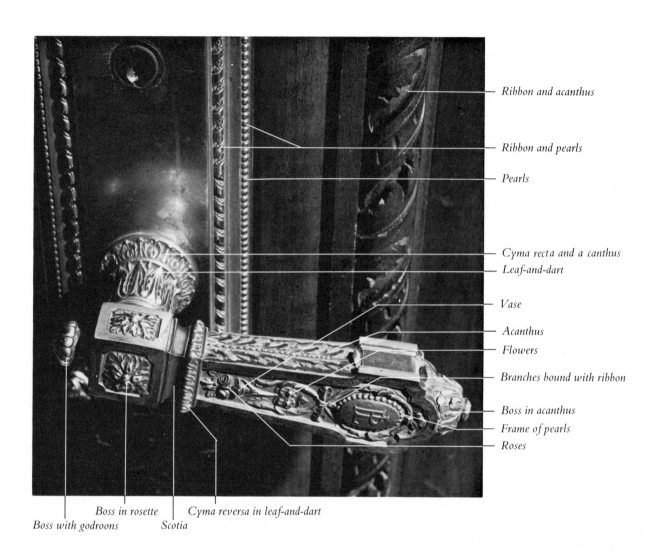

A lever handle of the door of the Trustees' Room

Ribbon and acanthus

Ribbon and pearls

Pearls

Cyma recta and a canthus

Leaf-and-dart

Vase

Acanthus

Flowers

Branches bound with ribbon

Boss in acanthus

Frame of pearls

Roses

Boss in rosette

Cyma reversa in leaf-and-dart

Boss with godroons

Scotia

The top of the Ionic pilaster and the enta-
blatures in the Trustees' Room

— *Cyma recta in leaf-and-dart*

— *Coffer*

— *Modillion in volute with acanthus*

— *Ovolo in egg-and-dart*

— *Bay leaves*
— *Scroll frame*
— *Pearls*
— *Fleur-de-lis*
— *Dolphin*
— *Crossed swords*

— *Cyma reversa in leaf-and-dart*

— *Fillet* ⎫
— *Cyma reversa in leaf-and-dart* ⎬ *Abacus*

— *Echinus in egg-and-dart*
— *Volute with acanthus*

— *Bead-and-reel*

— *Fluting on pilaster shaft*

2 5 7

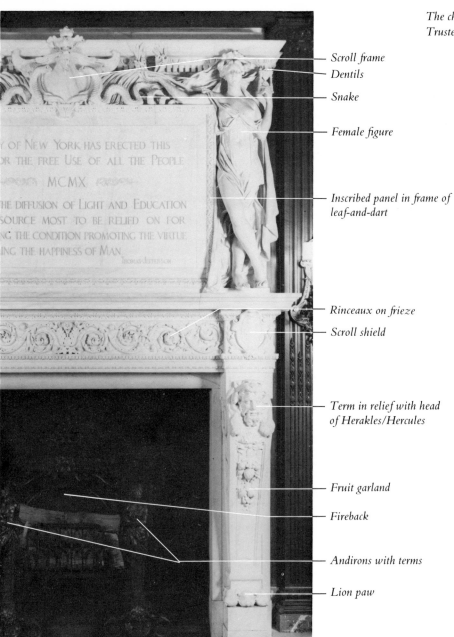

The chimneybreast and fireplace in the Trustees' Room

— Scroll frame
— Dentils

— Snake

— Female figure

— Inscribed panel in frame of leaf-and-dart

— Rinceaux on frieze
— Scroll shield

— Term in relief with head of Herakles/Hercules

— Fruit garland

— Fireback

— Andirons with terms

— Lion paw

Y OF NEW YORK HAS ERECTED THIS
OR THE FREE USE OF ALL THE PEOPLE
MCMX

THE DIFFUSION OF LIGHT AND EDUCATION
SOURCE MOST TO BE RELIED ON FOR
G THE CONDITION PROMOTING THE VIRTUE
ING THE HAPPINESS OF MAN
THOMAS JEFFERSON

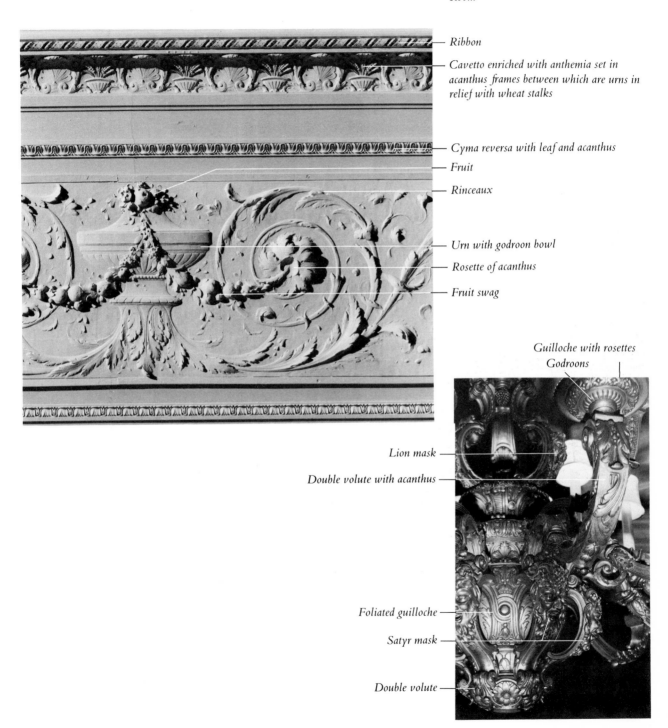

Ceiling ornament in the Trustees' Room
BELOW. The chandelier in the Trustees' Room

Ribbon

Cavetto enriched with anthemia set in acanthus frames between which are urns in relief with wheat stalks

Cyma reversa with leaf and acanthus

Fruit

Rinceaux

Urn with godroon bowl

Rosette of acanthus

Fruit swag

Guilloche with rosettes
Godroons

Lion mask

Double volute with acanthus

Foliated guilloche

Satyr mask

Double volute

The bronze door of the 42nd Street
Entrance

— Bead-and-reel

— Cloth swag with fluttering ribbon

— Books

— Lamp of learning

— Satyr mask

— Scroll frame with cabuchon

— Manuscripts

— Rinceaux with rosettes

— Vase

— Female figures in acanthus

— Plaque with scroll frame

— Satyr mask

— Fruit garland hanging from rinceaux

— Cyma reversa with anthemia, volutes in relief, and acanthus

— Bound bayleaves and bayberries on torus

— Boss with swirling acanthus leaves

— Bead-and-reel

— Cyma reversa with anthemia, volutes in relief, and acanthus

— Torus enriched with acorns and oak leaves

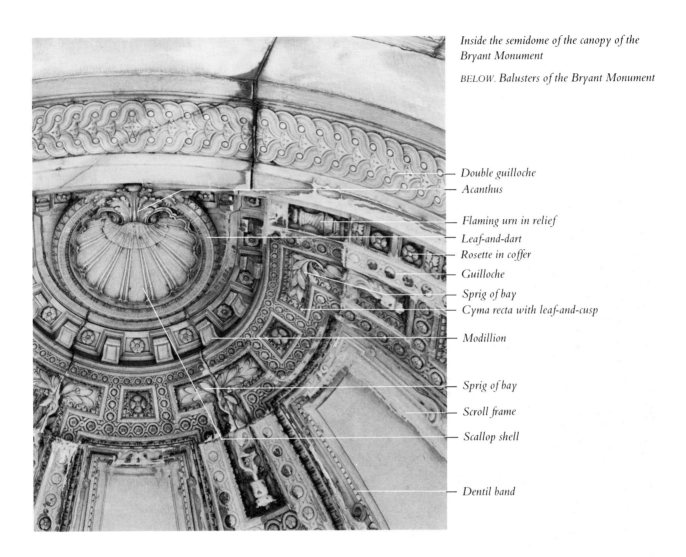

Inside the semidome of the canopy of the Bryant Monument

BELOW. Balusters of the Bryant Monument

Double guilloche
Acanthus

Flaming urn in relief
Leaf-and-dart
Rosette in coffer
Guilloche
Sprig of bay
Cyma recta with leaf-and-cusp

Modillion

Sprig of bay

Scroll frame

Scallop shell

Dentil band

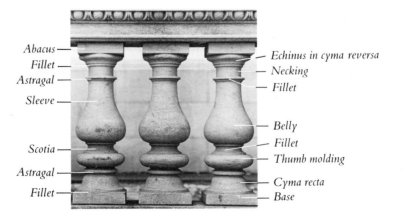

Abacus
Fillet
Astragal
Sleeve

Scotia

Astragal
Fillet

Echinus in cyma reversa
Necking
Fillet

Belly
Fillet
Thumb molding
Cyma recta
Base

COMPARISON OF ORDERS

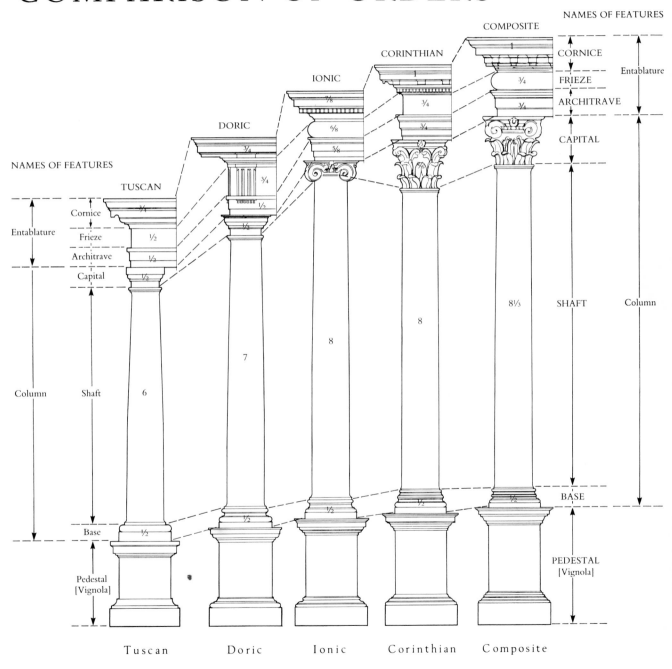

NAMES OF FEATURES

NAMES OF FEATURES

COMPOSITE

CORINTHIAN

IONIC

DORIC

TUSCAN

Cornice   ¾

Entablature

Frieze   ½

Architrave   ½

Capital   ½

Column

Shaft   6

Base   ½

Pedestal
[Vignola]

7

½

½

½

¾

¾

⅞

⁶⁄₈

⁵⁄₈

¾

8

½

8

¾

¾

¾

1

8

½

1

¾

¾

8⅓

½

CORNICE

Entablature

FRIEZE

ARCHITRAVE

CAPITAL

SHAFT   Column

BASE

PEDESTAL
[Vignola]

Tuscan   Doric   Ionic   Corinthian   Composite

263

ILLUSTRATED GLOSSARY OF ARCHITECTURAL AND DECORATIVE TERMS

Abacus. The slab that forms the top of the capital. *See* **Orders of architecture.**

Abutment. A masonry mass that takes the weight and thrust of an arch, vault or truss. See **Arch.**

Acanthus. A Mediterranean plant (Acanthus mollis and Acanthus spinosus) whose deeply serrated leaf was stylized by the Greeks and the Romans to become one of the principal ornaments of classical architecture. It identifies the Corinthian capital.

Acanthus spinosus   *Acanthus*

Aedicule. A small house or templed frame.

Ancone. A scroll-shaped bracket, customarily found in pairs, that supports a cornice over a door or a window. *See* **Bracket.**

Anthemion (anthemia, pl.) An ornament based on the honeysuckle or palm leaf. Also a Palmette.

Applique. See **Sconce.**

Arabesque. An intricate decorative pattern joining plant, animal, and sometimes human forms.

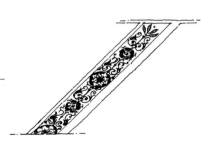

Arch. A curved construction used to span an opening or a recess.

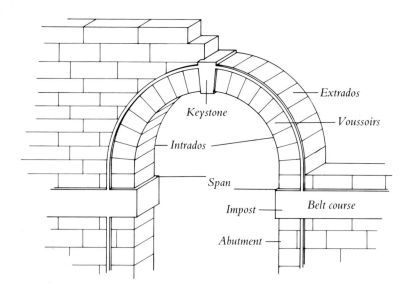

Architrave. The bottom third of the entablature, the part resting on the column or pilaster and supporting a frieze. It is often divided into fascia. *See* **Orders of architecture.**

Astragal. A small half-round to be seen on a capital. *See* **Orders of architecture** and **Moldings.** Also a molded strip applied to one side of a door leaf where the two leaves meet. It is designed to project over the adjoining leaf when the door is closed.

Attic. A story built above the cornice of a building.

Baluster. An upright support in a variety of turned shapes, customarily swelling toward the base. When one shape is inverted and superimposed on its model, it is called a double baluster. Used in a series

and supporting a rail, it forms part of a balustrade.

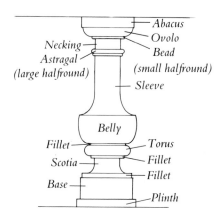

Barrel vault. A ceiling or roof construction as an extended arch over a space. Customarily semicyindrical in shape.

Base. The bottom part, made up of moldings, of the column and the pilaster, or of any architectural or

decorative design. *See* **Orders of architecture.**

Baseboard. A flat projection at the floor level of an interior wall. See **Dado.**

Batter. An incline given the face of a wall.

Bay, bayleaf, bayberry. A stylized leaf and berry of the bay tree, bay laurel or sweet bay (Laurus nobilis) often imbricated as in a wreath, in a swag, or in the enrichment of a torus.

Bead, bead molding. A small half-round. *See* **Moldings.**

Bead-and-reel. A molding made up of elongated beads and disks.

Beads. See **Pearls.**

Bed mold. The molding on which a cornice rests. *See* **Orders of architecture.**

Bel etage. The principal floor, customarily above the ground floor, reserved for reception rooms. Also Piano nobile.

Belt course. A horizontal band of masonry extending across the facade of a building. Also string course. *See* **Arch.**

Bezant. A coin-shaped ornament.

Bracket. A support for a projection, such as a cornice, usually scroll-shaped, as in a console bracket.

Bucrane. An ox skull. An ornamental device often used with garlands, festoons, and ribbons.

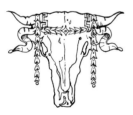

Cabuchon. A round or ovoid device with a convex surface, often elaborately framed. Also found in jewelry.

Caisson. A sunken panel in a vault or a dome. *See* **Coffer.**

Capital. The crowning member of a column or a pilaster. *See* **Orders of architecture.**

Cartouche. A shield or ovoid form often bearing inscriptions and devices in relief, frequently set in an elaborate scroll frame and bordered with ornament.

Cavetto. A concave molding with the profile of a quarter-round or close to it. *See* **Moldings.**

Chain band. A series of circles joined by paired hyphens, often with rosettes in the circles. When bordered by acanthus, it is known as a foliated chain band.

Coffer. A sunken panel in a ceiling, vault, or dome, or the underside of an arch. The great example of coffering is to be found in the Pantheon in Rome.

Column. A round, vertical support, consisting of a base, shaft, and capital, usually upholding an entablature. *See* **Orders of architecture.**

Console. A decorative bracket in the form of a scroll supporting a balcony, a table, or an overhanging wall.

Corinthian column. One of the five orders of columns mainly distinguished by its capital of acanthus leaves and volutes. It was the favorite order of the Romans. *See* **Orders of architecture.**

Cornice. The projecting top section of an entablature. *See* **Orders of architecture.**

Cornucopia. Also known as a Horn of Plenty, it is a goat's horn overflowing with fruit, grain, ears of corn, and similar items.

Corona. The flat part of a cornice between the cymatium above and the bed mold below. *See* **Orders of architecture.**

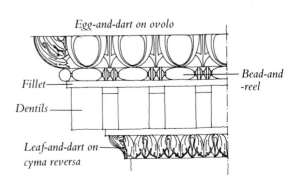

Egg-and-dart on ovolo

Fillet

Dentils

Bead-and-reel

Leaf-and-dart on cyma reversa

Course. A horizontal layer of masonry.

Cove. A concave surface connecting a ceiling and a wall.

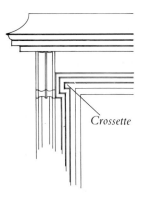

Crossette

Crossette. Also Greek Ear. A lateral extension of the architrave moldings at the top of a door or window frame.

Cyma recta. A molding with an S-shaped curve, concave over convex. *See* **Moldings.**

Cyma reversa. A molding with an S-shaped curve, convex over concave. *See* **Moldings.**

Cymatium. The uppermost molding of a cornice, usually in the shape of a cyma recta. *See* **Orders of architecture.**

Dado. A continuous wall pedestal or wainscot consisting of a base or baseboard, a die, and an upper rail or cap molding.

Dentil. A small projecting block used in rows, called a dentil band or course, forming part of a cornice. Dentils resemble teeth. *Denti-*

culated or *Denticular* means enriched with dentils. *See* **Cornice.**

Dome. A convex roof or ceiling, hemispherical, semiovoidal, or saucer-shaped, built over a square, octagonal, or circular space.

Doric column. One of the five orders of columns, with a simple capital consisting mainly of an abacus and echinus. *See* **Orders of architecture.**

Echinus. An ovolo or quarter-round molding that is part of a capital. *See* **Orders of architecture.**

Egg-and-dart. A familiar convex molding, an ovolo in profile enriched with eggs and arrowheads. *See* **Cornice.**

Entablature. The upper part of an order, supported by columns. Made up of three major horizontal members: architrave, frieze, and cornice. *See* **Orders of architecture.**

Entasis. An almost imperceptible swelling added to the tapering of the column shaft. It is a necessary refinement to correct the optical illusion of concavity that results if the column is straight.

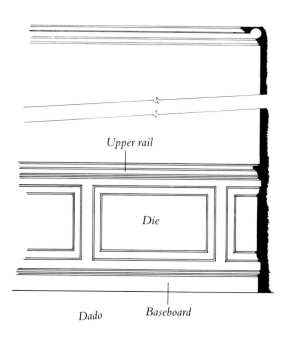

Upper rail

Die

Dado   Baseboard

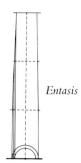

Entasis

Extrados. The outside surface of an arch. *See* **Arch.**

Fascia. The plain horizontal band or bands, often combined with moldings, that make up the architrave, the lowest, third part of the entablature. *See* **Orders of architecture.**

Festoon. A garland made of fruits, flowers, leaves, or husks, and hanging in a curve. Alternative term: Swag. *Also see* **Garland.**

Fillet. A raised, narrow flat band between the flutes of a column. Also a raised or sunken band when combined with other elements. *See* **Moldings.**

Fleuron. A small flower-shaped ornament usually found on the abacus of a Corinthian column. *See* **Orders of architecture,** Corinthian.

Flute. A concave groove or channel running vertically on a column or pilaster shaft. Also found in enriched moldings. Collectively called fluting.

Fluttering ribbon. (See illustration.)

Fret. A geometrical meandering pattern of horizontal and vertical straight lines making a band. Also called Greek key.

Frieze. The middle horizontal member of an entablature above the architrave and below the cornice. *See* **Orders of architecture.**

Garland. An intertwining of fruits, leaves, flowers, or husks.

Godroon. Old spelling, gadroon. A convex rounded ornament, always in a set; for that reason, most often called godroons. The godroon is round at the upper end and tapering to a point at the other.

Groin. The ridge at the intersection of two vaults. A groined vault.

Guilloche. An ornament composed of continuous interlaced curving lines. When there are two linked patterns, it is known as a double guilloche.

Fret

Guttae. A series of cone-shaped or cylindrical pendants on the underside of a triglyph. *See* **Orders of architecture.**

Helix. The volutes or scrolls of a Corinthian capital. *See* **Orders of architecture,** Corinthian.

Imbricated. A pattern of overlapping leaves or scales, usually of bay leaves, oak leaves, or bezants. *Imbrication:* a band of the same.

Impost. A cornicelike bracket from which an arch springs. Also called impost block. *See* **Arch.**

Ionic. One of the five orders of columns, recognized by its capital of volutes or helixes. *See* **Orders of architecture.**

Jib door. A door made to look indistinguishable from the wall in which it stands.

Keystone. The wedged top stone of an arch. *See* **Arch.**

Leaf-and-dart. A repetitive band made up of a stylized leaf and a dart. Sometimes called water leaf, a term invented by an 18th-century archaeologist.

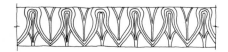

Lintel. A horizontal member spanning an opening as in a door or a window.

Lunette. A semicircular wall inside an arch. Often applied to a painting that fills the same.

Meander. *See* **Fret.**

Metope. A square panel between triglyphs on a Doric frieze. Often decorated with a relief. *See* **Orders of architecture,** Doric.

Modillion. A small bracket used in rows under the corona of a cornice and extending from the bed mold. It frequently takes the shape of an ornamental double volute.

Moldings. Plain or decorated surfaces either rectangular or curved and either above or below the surface. Their purpose is to provide a transition or to produce light and shade.

Monolith. The shaft of a column consisting of a single block of stone. Also monolithic.

Necking. Also known as collarino, a wide surface at the top of a Tuscan, Doric, or Ionic column. *See* **Orders of architecture.**

Niche. A recess in a wall, usually with a semidome, designed as a place for a statue.

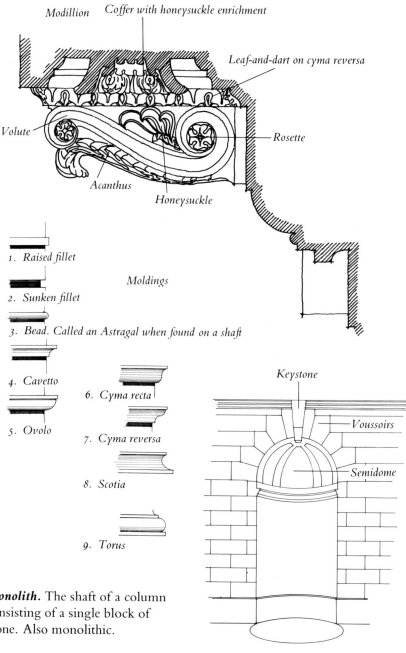

Modillion   Coffer with honeysuckle enrichment

Leaf-and-dart on cyma reversa

Volute

Rosette

Acanthus

Honeysuckle

1. *Raised fillet*

Moldings

2. *Sunken fillet*

3. *Bead. Called an Astragal when found on a shaft*

4. *Cavetto*

5. *Ovolo*

6. *Cyma recta*

7. *Cyma reversa*

8. *Scotia*

9. *Torus*

Keystone

Voussoirs

Semidome

Niche

Orders of architecture (Five Orders). An order consists of a column with base (except in the Greek Doric), shaft, and capital and its entablature. Each order has its own formalized ornament. The orders are the basis of architectural design in the classical tradition, providing lessons in proportion, scale, and the uses of ornament. The five orders are Tuscan, Doric, Ionic, Corinthian, and Composite.

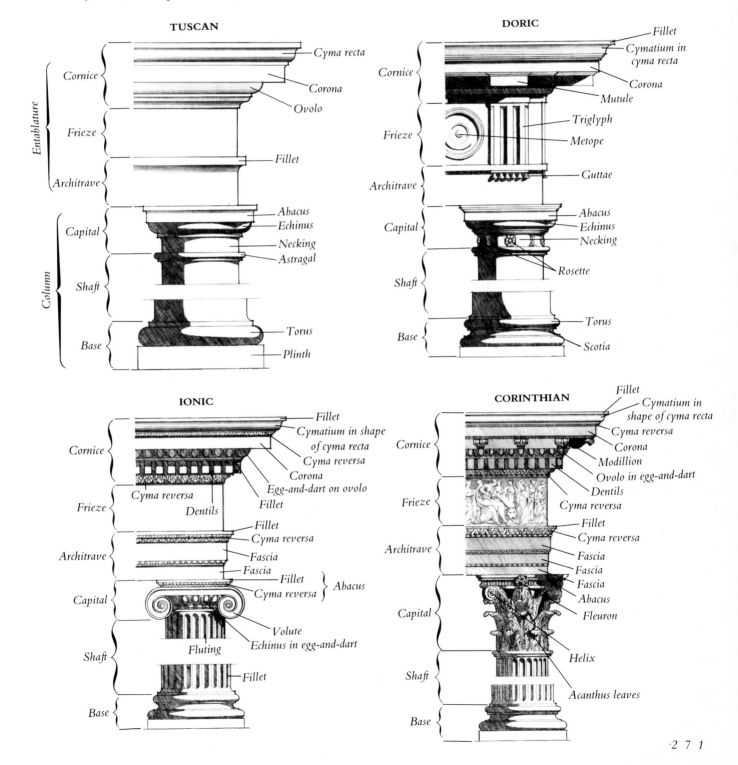

TUSCAN

Entablature
Cornice
— Cyma recta
— Corona
— Ovolo

Frieze

Architrave
— Fillet

Column
Capital
— Abacus
— Echinus
— Necking
— Astragal

Shaft

Base
— Torus
— Plinth

DORIC

Cornice
— Fillet
— Cymatium in cyma recta
— Corona
— Mutule

Frieze
— Triglyph
— Metope

Architrave
— Guttae

Capital
— Abacus
— Echinus
— Necking

Shaft
— Rosette

Base
— Torus
— Scotia

IONIC

Cornice
— Fillet
— Cymatium in shape of cyma recta
— Cyma reversa
— Corona
— Egg-and-dart on ovolo
— Fillet

Cyma reversa
Dentils

Frieze

Architrave
— Fillet
— Cyma reversa
— Fascia
— Fascia

Capital
— Fillet
— Cyma reversa } Abacus
— Volute
— Echinus in egg-and-dart

Shaft
Fluting

Base
— Fillet

CORINTHIAN

Fillet
Cymatium in shape of cyma recta
Cyma reversa
Corona
Modillion
Ovolo in egg-and-dart
Dentils
Cyma reversa

Cornice

Frieze

Architrave
— Fillet
— Cyma reversa
— Fascia
— Fascia
— Fascia
— Abacus
— Fleuron

Capital
— Helix

Shaft
— Acanthus leaves

Base

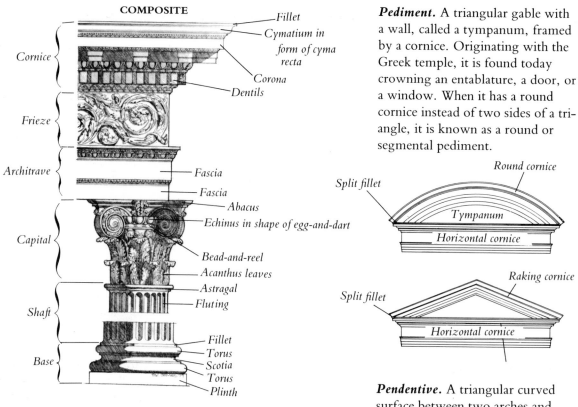

COMPOSITE

Fillet

Cymatium in form of cyma recta

Cornice

Corona

Dentils

Frieze

Architrave

Fascia

Fascia

Abacus

Echinus in shape of egg-and-dart

Capital

Bead-and-reel

Acanthus leaves

Astragal

Fluting

Shaft

Fillet

Torus

Scotia

Base

Torus

Plinth

Pediment. A triangular gable with a wall, called a tympanum, framed by a cornice. Originating with the Greek temple, it is found today crowning an entablature, a door, or a window. When it has a round cornice instead of two sides of a triangle, it is known as a round or segmental pediment.

Round cornice

Split fillet

Tympanum

Horizontal cornice

Raking cornice

Split fillet

Horizontal cornice

Ovolo. A convex molding, either elliptical or quarter-round. *See* **Moldings.**

Patera (paterae, pl.). An ornament, usually in the form of a rosette, to be found in coffers.

Palmette. *See* **Anthemion.**

Pearls. A small molding resembling a string of pearls. Also known as beads.

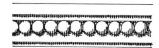

Pedestal. A base for a column, pilaster, or statue. Also a post in a balustrade. *See* **Balustrade.**

Pendentive. A triangular curved surface between two arches and beneath a dome.

Piano nobile. *See* **Bel etage.**

Pier. A heavy vertical mass of masonry used for support with none of the details of a column.

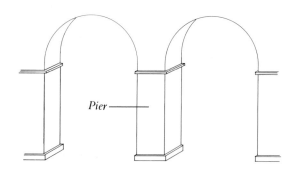

Pier

Pilaster. A vertical rectangular projection from a wall, treated like a column with base, shaft, and capital.

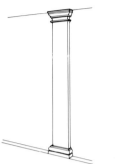

Plinth. An additional base beneath the base of a column, or pilaster, or baluster. A *plinth course* is a continuous plinth serving as base to a number of columns, pilasters or balusters (balustrade).

Post. An upright supporting member.

Pulvinated. Pillow-shaped, as in the curved profile of a frieze, such as in a pulvinated frieze. It is also found in rustication where the stones are given a pillow shape.

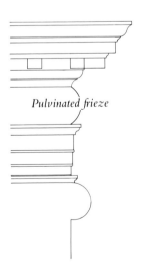

Pulvinated frieze

Raking cornice. Sloping cornice of the two sides of a pediment. *See* **Pediment.**

Reed. A bead or beaded molding, i.e., a small half-round. When used in clusters it is called *reeding*.

Reveal. The section of the wall framing a window or a door, customarily when the wall is thick.

Ribbon. An ornament in imitation of a cloth ribbon.

Rinceau (rinceaux, pl.). A symmetrical swirling ornament of leaves, customarily those of the acanthus.

Rosette. A floral motive, usually round. Paterae in coffers are most often in the shape of rosettes.

Rostrum (rostra, pl.). The prow of a Greek or Roman warship used as a ram in battle. Stone imitations of them are part of the grammar of classical ornament and are customarily found on columns. Captured rostra were placed at the foot of the speaker's podium in the Roman Forum; for that reason such a podium is called a rostrum.

Rustication, rusticated. The name for cut stone in a wall that is channeled with grooves. The purpose is to convey an impression of solidity and strength and to give visual relief to the wall surface.

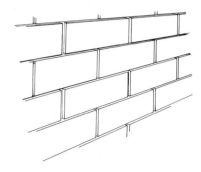

Saucer dome. A low concave ceiling, with the shape of an inverted saucer.

Sconce. A bracket, secured to a wall, with a candlestick or several candlesticks, or imitations of same, or with arms holding lights. Also known as Applique.

Scroll. A spiral found in the form of volutes of a capital or in the frame of a cartouche.

Scroll frame. A frame adorned with scrolls that looks as if it were made of thick boiled leather.

Segmental. The portion of a circle, less than a semicircle, defining the shape of an arch or a vault.

Shaft. The trunk or the longest part of a column between the base and the capital. *See* **Orders of architecture.**

Soffit. The underside of an arch, a beam, or any spanning member. *See* **Arch.**

Spandrel. The triangular space bounded by the curve of an arch, a horizontal line through its top, and a vertical line rising from the impost or springing of the arch.

Splay. A sloped surface, usually in the arch of a door or window where one side is larger than the other.

Split fillet. A fillet found on the horizontal and raking cornices of a pediment, termed split because it divides at an angle where the two cornices meet. *See* **Pediment.**

Stereotomy, stereotomic. The science and art of stone cutting.

Stopped fluting. Where the flutes or channels of a column or pilaster, or any grooves, have been filled with rods or rods topped by acanthus.

Strapwork. A form of ornamentation consisting of folding and interlacing bands.

String course or belt course. A horizontal band across a facade. It can be flush or projecting, and given a variety of surfaces.

Swag. *See* **Festoon.**

Taenia. The fillet at the top of a Doric architrave. *See* **Orders of architecture,** DORIC.

Thumb molding. Also known as a quirked molding. In profile it is part round and part elliptical.

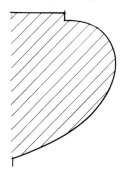

Triglyph. A projecting block with three channels forming part of a Doric frieze. *See* **Orders of Architecture,** DORIC.

Vault. An arched ceiling.

Vestibule. An anteroom, entrance hall, or foyer.

Volute. A spiral scroll as on an Ionic, Corinthian, or Composite capital, or any spiral ornament. Also known as helix. *See* **Orders of architecture.**

The GLOSSARY is based on *The American Vignola* by William R. Ware, a Classical America Series book. For help in the definitions, the author is indebted to Dr. Richard H. Howland, to James Parker of the Metropolitan Museum of Art, and to Alvin Holm, President of the Philadelphia Chapter of Classical America. The drawings were executed by Alvin Holm, Cameron MacTavish, Harvey Heiser, David R. Kulick, Steven W. Semes, Michael Javelos, and Stephen Wright.

APPENDICES

Building Statistics of the Main Research Library of the New York Public Library

	SQUARE FEET
Cellar	90,270
Basement	88,697
Stack 2	23,760
First Floor	81,544
Stack 4	23,760
Mezzanine	8,220
Stack 5	23,760
Second Floor	81,544
Stack 7	23,760
Third Floor	81,544
Total	526,859

APPENDIX II   VARIETIES OF STONE IN THE NEW YORK PUBLIC LIBRARY

A list of most of the varieties of stone to be found in the New York Public Library. Compiled with the help of the authority on the building stone of New York, Sidney Horenstein, Invertebrate Paleontologist, American Museum of Natural History, and Professor John Patton, State Geologist, State of Indiana

COLOR AND PLACE	NAME	SOURCE
Orange granite curbing	Stony Creek	Stony Creek Area on Leetes Island, east of New Haven, Conn.
Also found at the Grand Central Terminal and the base of the Statue of Liberty		
Gunmetal bluestone in big slabs on the sidewalk	Hudson River	Catskill Mountains, New York State
Formerly the best material for sidewalks. Also seen in front of St. Thomas Church on Fifth Avenue and 53rd Street		
Gray granite in the Terrace balustrade	Milford	Milford, Mass.
Cream, pale pink marble in lions, flag-pole bases and Bryant Monument	Tennessee Pink or Tennessee/Knoxville	Near Knoxville, Tenn.
Floor of Grand Central Terminal and facade of National Gallery of Art in Washington		
Vases	Knoxville Gray	Near Knoxville, Tenn.
White marble ranging from almost pure white to white with dark streaks	Danby/Dorset	From Dorset Mountain near Danby (Manchester) Vermont
Found in the Soldiers and Sailors Monument on Riverside Drive, New York City		
Mottled gray marble with patches of yellow in floors	Gray Siena	Montarenti, Siena, Italy
Beige marble in floors	Hauteville	Hauteville-Lompnès Department of Ain, France
Walls of the Roosevelt Memorial and corridors, American Museum of Natural History		
Cloudy white marble on walls	Pentelic	Mount Pentelikon outside of Athens, Greece
The Marble of the Parthenon		
Dark gray marble for door frames	Formosa	Wetzlar, Nassau, Germany
Only fossiliferous stone in the library. It contains Stromatoporoids, sponge-like creatures.		
Dark green marble in table bases	Verde Antique	Roxbury, Vermont
Mottled purplish marble in floor borders	Red Champlain, "Oriental Variety"	Swanton, Vermont
Found in the floor of Stairway Hall in the Library of Congress and at entrance to Century Association, New York City		
Mottled soft red marble in doorway frames and wall bases	Rouge Jaspe	Near Toulon, Department of Var, France
Pure white marble of candelabra. Also found in the restrooms	White Italian Bianco P	Near Carrara, Apennine Alps, Italy
Black inset in panels of Gray Siena in Second Floor fountain	Belgian Black	Mazy, Namur, Belgium

Marble panels on east wall of Trustees' Room		
Yellow panel	Yellow Siena	Montarenti, Siena, Italy
Green inset	Verde Antique	Roxbury, Vermont
Purple marble in narrow panels	Breche violette	Lake Garda, Italy
Black marble with gray and gold streaks found on tops of console tables in Trustees' Room	Black Gold	Porto Venere, Italy
White marble of chimney breast in Trustees' Room	Eastman Cream	West Rutland, Vermont
Dark gray basalt in steps and landing of 42nd Street Entrance	French Creek Granite, not a granite but a basalt	French Creek, Pennsylvania
Yellow marble panels in Room 80	Yellow Siena	Montarenti, Siena, Italy

ADDENDUM

Stone used in 1985 restsoration of the Library Terrace. (Information from Ellen L. Albert of Davis, Brody & Assocs.)

COLOR AND PLACE	NAME	SOURCE
Gray granite on Terrace	Chelmsford	Chelmsford, Massachusetts
Gray granite in Terrace balustrade	Milford	Milford, Massachusetts
Bluestone on Terrace	Elk Brook	East Branch, New York
White marble on stairway of Fifth Avenue Entrance	Plateau Danby	Proctor, Vermont

APPENDIX III MAJOR DONORS TO THE LIBRARY

Major Donors to the Library As Listed in Astor Hall

APPENDIX IV   LIBRARY STAFF WHO SERVED IN WORLD WARS I AND II

Members of the Library Staff Who Served in World War I and World War II Listed on Bronze Plaques on the Wall to the Left of the Door to the Gottesman Exhibition Hall

*Died in Service

WORLD WAR I

*William Berthold Behrens   *Robert Shevitt

George Appold	Waldo W. Gower	Carl F. Peehl
John Archer	Fred G. Harman	Oscar Perlstein
Millard Blanchard	Martin F. Hession	Charles H. Reinert
Donald K. Campbell	Anne A. Kilcourse	Paul North Rice
Carl L. Cannon	Otto Kinkeldey	Gustav G. Rosenberg
Edward H. Collins	Karl H. Koopman	J. Louis Rosenbergen
John J. Collins	Thomas J. McCarrick	Fred C. Schilling
William Cordez	Nelson W. McCombs	Kai Schwensen
Francis Daly	John S. R. McDonald	Philip B. Scott
G. Blaine Darrah	William McMahon	Thomas G. Shafer
George C. Davies	Nellie Mahoney	Abraham Shampanier
Francis J. Dolezal	John Maier	Charles Spuhr
Isidore Drabskin	Louis Marangella	James E. Sterritt
Lawrence Fassig	Charles E. Mang	Alex Uhl
John C. Frank	William J. Mang	Robert W. G. Vail
C. Wallace French	Richard Meyer	John Vierow
Carl O. Gistedt	Nicholas J. Morales	John T. Wade
Ethel Goldsmith	Hugo Mortzsch	
Hugh Gordon	Edmund Lester Pearson	

WORLD WAR II

Frederick A. Abben	Bernard P. Barry	Robert Blackman
Gordon C. Abrams	Richard E. Baum	Keith G. Blair
John Alexander	Harold Beach	William Bollman, III
Marion N. Allan	Leo Beck	Marion E. Bonniwell
Robert R. Ansell	Sidney Beck	Frederick V. Borgen
Albert Antenucci	Theodore Beck	William R. Brandt
Kenneth Appell	Nancy Bedell	Peter Brescia
Samuel Baig	Judah Berger	Alfred Bresiger
Dorothy Bamber	Joseph Bernstein	Albert Brianzi
Arthur J. Barnett	Myron Bichler	Johnnie Brown

Lawrence Byrnes
Francis J. Calabro
Gilbert A. Cam
★John Carhuff
★Elliott Carmen
Joseph H. Carroll
John Casey
Moreau B. Chambers
Joseph P. Charles
William T. Cheswell
Jean E. Child
Frank Christiana
Charles J. Churgin
Gerald W. Clifford
Patrick J. Cloonan
Irwin Cohen
Mortimer Cohen
Charles Comerford
John R. Courtney
Raymond Currier
Benjamin Cushing
Alfred D'Addario
Alexander Dalin
Leo D'Arrigo
John Dawson
Michael De Felice
John Delaney
Joseph De Mascio
★Edward De Simone
Archibald P. De Weese
Ernest E. Doerschuk
Eugene Donohue
Charles E. Dornbusch
James A. Douglas
Thomas Dunn
Thomas J. Egan, Jr.
Paul Ehrlich
William J. Elliott
Philip Elson
Mary Emerson
Joseph H. Engel
Donald B. Engley
Raymond Faber
Ebbe Fangel
Frank Fardellone
Edward Feihel
Thomas A. Fogarty
Frank J. Foley
Roger B. Francis

Sidney M. Frank
Paul Gainor
Lawrence Garavante
Martin L. Garry
John A. Gault
Walter N. Gelby
John Georgopulos
Jerome Ghimassi
Frank Giacinto
James H. Gibson
Adrian T. Gilmore
Jack Goldstein
John D. Gordan
Herbert L. Gordon
Jerald Gorman
Angelo Granatelli
George R. Guinazzo
John P. Hackett
Charles T. Haffey
Michael P. Hearn
Jacob Heller
Howard Henke, Jr.
John O. Herr
Su Chen Ho
★Charles E. Hough
James Humphry, III
John Hutson
Milton Imberman
William A. Jefsen
Albert Johnson
Harold Jones
Andrew Kalfas
Eugene D. Kaptein
Xavier Kaptein
Leon Karpel
★Howard Kelly
Edward Kennedy
Thomas F. Kennedy, Jr.
Thomas V. Kenny
Robert J. Kerrigan
Richard Kimmerer
Robert E. Kingery
Harold J. Koeffler
Harold Kropitzer
Edward J. Kruger
Karl Kup
Peter J. Lally
Gustave Lamm
John T. Landers

James G. Law
Marjorie Learned
William J. Leavey
Leonard S. Lee
William P. Leonard
Paulene Lewis
David Libbey
John J. Litz
Martin L. Loftus
Thomas P. Lynch
Charles N. MacKenzie
Alex Manzinos
Dvoichenko Markov
Joseph Mazzu
Gerald D. McDonald
William McInerney
Philip McIntosh
Kurt Melinger
John Mertz
Philip Miller
Philip Miner
Hugh Montgomery
George Moriarty
Wilfred L. Morin
Edward B. Morrison
Martin Morrison
Denys P. Myers, Jr.
Charles Neldner
Richard Nowell
Joseph Novotny
John J. O'Loughlin, Jr.
William Orth
Steven S. Pappas
Joseph Pascale
Harry Perkins
Anthony Perrone
Matthew Piana
A. W. H. Pilkington
Stanley R. Pillsbury
Dawn Pohlman
Joseph Pompilio, Jr.
George C. Poock
Irving Portnoy
Donald M. Powell
Joseph Prince
Donald R. Prismon
Howard C. Reuter
Saro J. Riccardi
Ira C. Robbins

Augustine Romano
Donald F. Rossler
Edith Russell
Francis R. St. John
Ralph Savio
August Schaefer
Alfred Schorr
Benjamin Schwartz
Philip Sciortino
Frank K. Seegraber
Helen A. Shenitz
Edward L. Shields
Walter J. Shoopinsky
Morris Slotkin
Hal H. Smith
Lawrence V. Snyder
Donald E. Soergel
Leonard Sommer
Berthold Sorbey
Chester M. Southam

Richard N. Stern
Robert Stevens
William F. Stewart
John R. Stoehr, Jr.
Daniel J. Sughrue
Edith Sullivan
Edward Sweekly
Albert Templeton
David Thomas
Janet Thomas
Lewis Thompson
Elias Throne
James G. Tobin
Frank Tomasino
James Tonrey
John Vasicek
Lewis D. Vickers
Lucian Visintin
Paul Von Khrum

Seymour Wald
Audrey Walker
Charles Walpole
Patrick Ward
Fritz Weinschenk
Morris Weitman
Bernard Wengrover
★Joseph T. Wheeler
Robert C. Wilkinson
Katherine Winter
Louis Woebse
Bernard Wolzer
Charles S. Woodbury
Max Yablon
Irving Zand
Josef Zatzkis
Frank Zika
Alexander Zoueff
Eugene D. Zweig

APPENDIX V   FOUNDING LIFE CONSERVATORS AND LIFE CONSERVATORS

Founding Life Conservators and Life Conservators As Listed on the West of the 42nd Street Entrance

FOUNDING LIFE CONSERVATORS

Family of Nelson I. Asiel
Brooke Russell Astor
Alice K. Bache
George F. Baker Trust
Howard Bayne Fund
Carrie S. Beinecke
Stephen and Mary Birch Foundation
Edith C. Blum Foundation
Margaret L. Brown
Helen Watson Buckner
Mr. & Mrs. Chester F. Carlson
Mrs. Gilbert W. Chapman
Mrs. Percy Chubb
Clark Foundation
Peter C. Cornell Trust
Lillian Cossow
Mr. & Mrs. Edgar W. Couper
Patricia Pogue & Richard W. Couper
Mary W. Covington
Mina K. Curtiss
Rita M. Cushman
Mr. & Mrs. Jean Delmas
The Cleveland H. Dodge Foundation, Inc.

Ruth W. Dolen Foundation
The Doris Duke Foundation
The Caleb C. and Julia W. Dula Educational
    and Charitable Foundation
The Charles Engelhard Foundation
Mrs. Richard P. Ettinger
Ruth Page Fisher
Ruby B. Fleming
Mr. & Mrs. Wm. Ward Foshay
Mr. & Mrs. William T. Golden
Mrs. John D. Gordan
The Gramercy Park Foundation
The Green Fund, Inc.
Mary Livingston Griggs and Mary Griggs
    Burke Foundation
Paul A. Guibert
Thomas A. Guinzburg
John H. Gutfreund
Stella and Charles Guttman Foundation, Inc.
Katherine B. Hadley
Mr. & Mrs. Ralph E. Hansmann
W. Averell Harriman
In Memory of Ruth F. Hays
Joseph H. Hazen

Hess Foundation, Inc.
Mr. & Mrs. Theodore S. Hope, Jr.
Josephine Lawrence Hopkins Foundation
The Ittleson Foundation
The J. M. Foundation
Christian A. Johnson Endeavor Foundation
The J. M. Kaplan Fund
Mrs. Artemis Karagheusian
Mr. & Mrs. Finbar Kenny
Lincoln Kirstein
Lawrence Klosk
Olga Knoepke
Jeanette Labelson
Dr. & Mrs. Edwin H. Land
Roy E. Larsen
Lewis F. Lehrman
Barbara Levy
Leon Levy
Harold E. Linder
Vera & Albert A. List
John E. Lockwood
James A. Macdonald Foundation
In Loving Memory of Nancy G. MacGrath
Abby R. Mauze

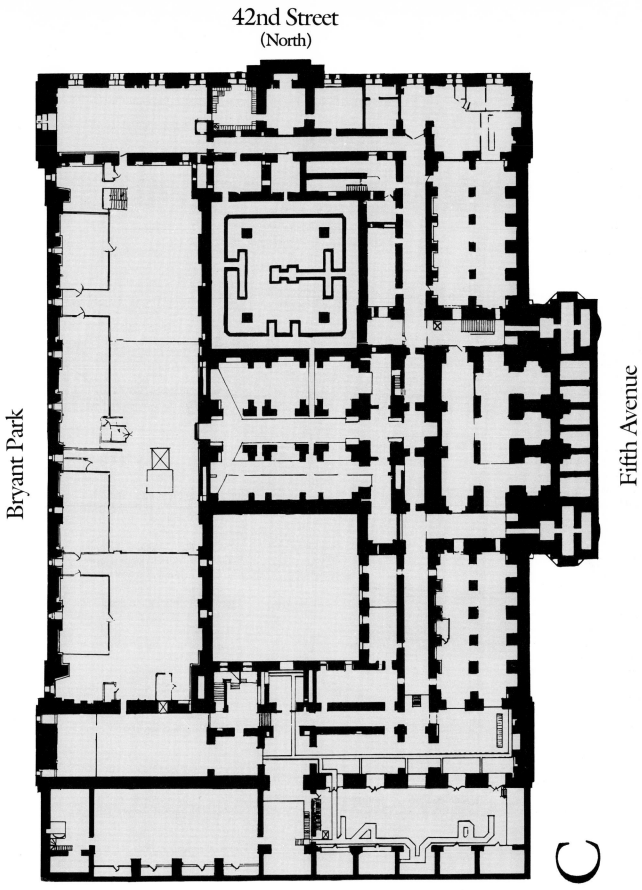

42nd Street
(North)

40th Street
(South)

Bryant Park

Fifth Avenue

The New York Public Library Cellar

Cellar Closed to the Public

C

283

42nd Street
(North)

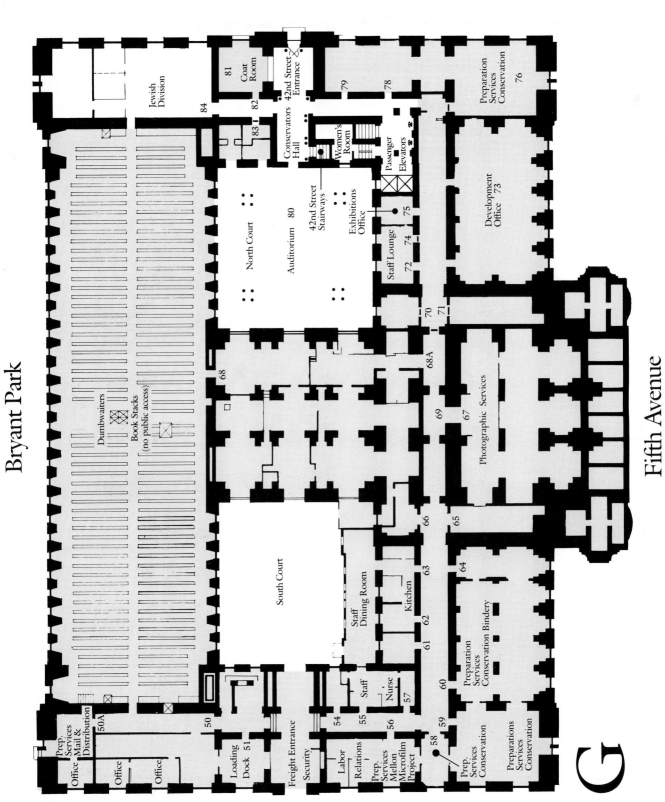

Bryant Park

Fifth Avenue

The New York Public Library Ground Floor

G

Shaded Areas Closed to the Public

40th Street
(South)

42nd Street
(North)

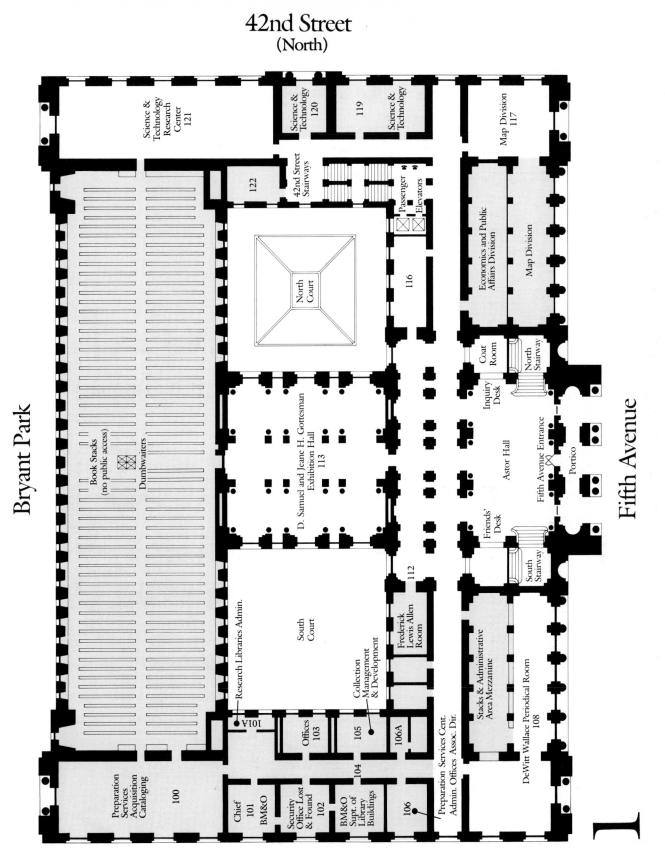

Bryant Park

Fifth Avenue

40th Street
(South)

Science & Technology Research Center 121

Science & Technology 120

119

Science & Technology

Map Division 117

122

42nd Street Stairways

North Court

Passenger Elevators

116

Economics and Public Affairs Division

Map Division

Book Stacks (no public access)

Dumbwaiters

Coat Room

North Stairway

Inquiry Desk

D. Samuel and Jeane H. Gottesman Exhibition Hall 113

Astor Hall

Fifth Avenue Entrance

Portico

Friends' Desk

South Court

Research Libraries Admin.

Collection Management & Development

South Stairway

101A

Offices 103

105

106A

Frederick Lewis Allen Room

112

Preparation Services Acquisition Cataloging

100

Stacks & Administrative Area Mezzanine

DeWitt Wallace Periodical Room 108

Chief 101 BM&O

Security Office Lost & Found 102

BM&O Supt. of Library Buildings

104

106

Preparation Services Cent. Admin. Offices Assoc. Dir.

The New York Public Library First Floor

Shaded Areas Closed to the Public

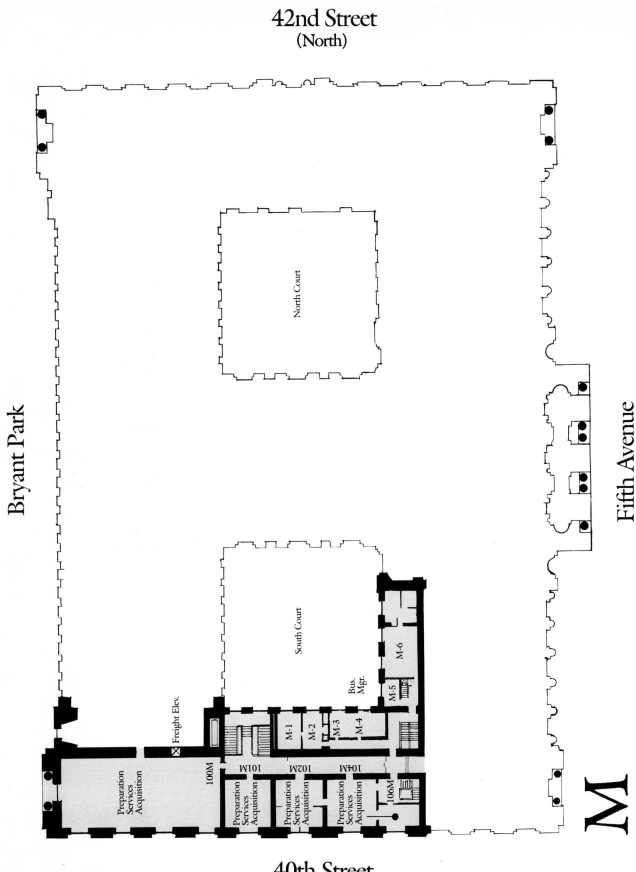

42nd Street
(North)

40th Street
(South)

Bryant Park

Fifth Avenue

North Court

South Court

Preparation Services Acquisition

100M

101M

102M

104M

106M

Preparation Services Acquisition

Preparation Services Acquisition

Preparation Services Acquisition

Freight Elev.

M-1

M-2

M-3

M-4

M-5

M-6

Bus. Mgr.

M

The New York Public Library Mezzanine Floor

Shaded Areas Closed to the Public

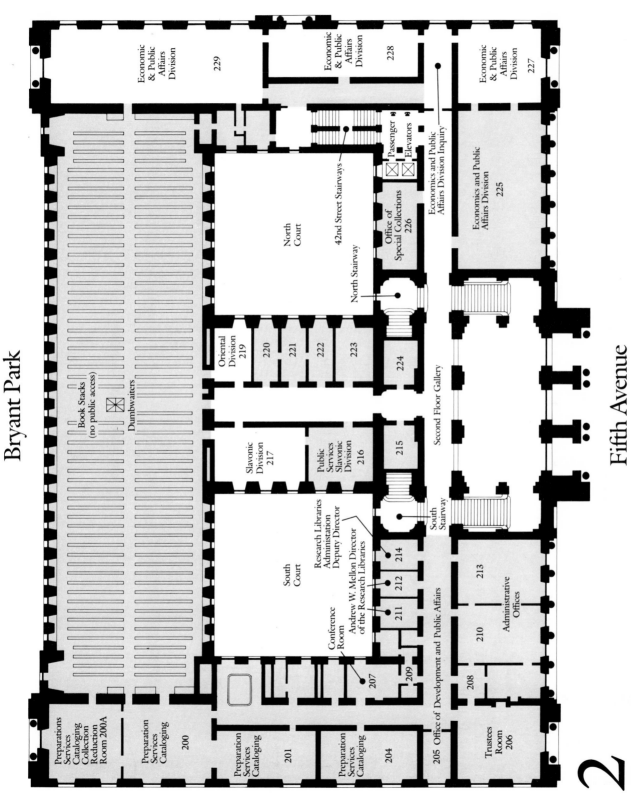

42nd Street
(North)

Bryant Park

Fifth Avenue

40th Street
(South)

The New York Public Library Second Floor

Shaded Areas Closed to the Public

2

Economic & Public Affairs Division
229

Economic & Public Affairs Division
228

Economic & Public Affairs Division
227

North Court

42nd Street Stairways

Passenger Elevators

Economics and Public Affairs Division Inquiry

Office of Special Collections
226

Economics and Public Affairs Division
225

North Stairway

Preparations Services Cataloging Collection Reduction Room 200A

Preparation Services Cataloging
200

Book Stacks (no public access)

Dumbwaiters

Oriental Division
219

220

221

222

223

224

Second Floor Gallery

Slavonic Division
217

Public Services Slavonic Division
216

215

Preparation Services Cataloging
201

Preparation Services Cataloging
204

South Court

Conference Room

Research Libraries Administration Deputy Director

Andrew W. Mellon Director of the Research Libraries

207

211

212

214

South Stairway

209

205 Office of Development and Public Affairs

208

210

213

Administrative Offices

Trustees Room
206

2 8 7

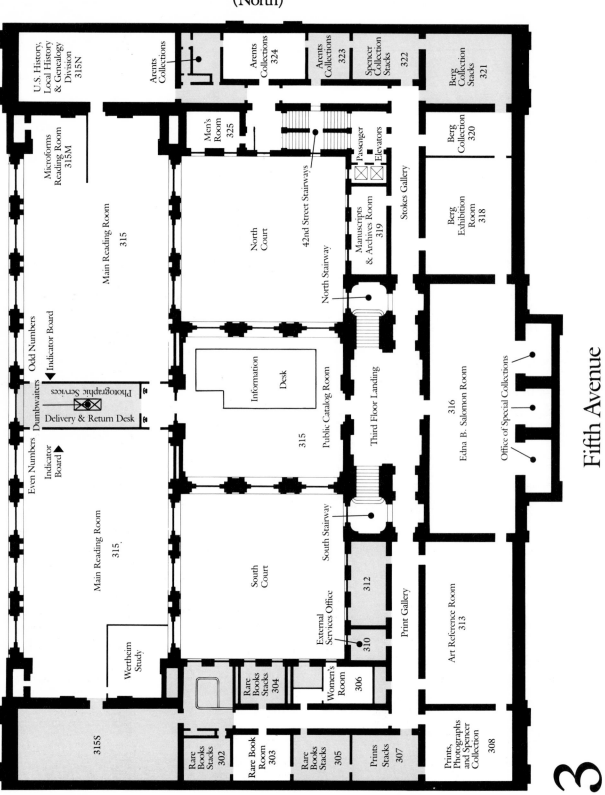

42nd Street
(North)

Bryant Park

U.S. History, Local History & Genealogy Division 315N

Microforms Reading Room 315M

Main Reading Room 315

Odd Numbers ▼Indicator Board

Photographic Services

Dumbwaiters

Even Numbers ▲ Indicator Board

Delivery & Return Desk

Main Reading Room 315

Wertheim Study

315S

Arents Collections

Arents Collections 324

Arents Collections 323

Spencer Collection Stacks 322

Berg Collection Stacks 321

Men's Room 325

42nd Street Stairways

Passenger Elevators

Stokes Gallery

Berg Collection 320

North Court

Manuscripts & Archives Room 319

Berg Exhibition Room 318

North Stairway

Information Desk

Public Catalog Room 315

Third Floor Landing

Office of Special Collections

Edna B. Salomon Room 316

South Stairway

South Court

External Services Office

312

Print Gallery

310

Art Reference Room 313

Rare Books Stacks 304

Women's Room

306

Rare Books Stacks 302

Rare Book Room 303

Rare Books Stacks 305

Prints Stacks 307

Prints, Photographs and Spencer Collection 308

Fifth Avenue

The New York Public Library Third Floor

3

■ Shaded Areas Closed to the Public

40th Street
(South)

INDEX

Adams, Herbert, 29, 188, 204, 210
Aldrich, Chester, 23
Alexander, John W., 133
Allen, Frederick Lewis, Room, 76
American Vignola, The, 8, 19, 65, 173
André, Pierre, 20
Architects' Emergency Committee, 210
Architectural Record, 14
Arents Collection, 32, 128
Arents, George, 128
Areopagitica (Milton), 145
Argonauts (Jason), 41
Arlington Memorial Amphitheatre, 30
Arnold Constable Store, 32
Art Nouveau, 162
Art Reference Room, 129
Astor, Brooke Russell, 111, 196
Astor Reading Room, 163
Astor Hall, xi, 14, 16, 65–72, 114, 122, 125, 200
Astor, John Jacob, 3, 4, 16, 48, 112, 163, 184
Astor, John Jacob III, 167
Astor, William Backhouse I, 166
Avery, Samuel Putnam, 29

Badgeley, Clarence Dale, 210
Bakewell & Brown, 122
Barber, Donn, 23
Barnard, George Grey, 23, 28, 53, 54, 55
Bartlett, Paul Wayland, 28, 48
Bayley, John Barrington, N.3, 18, 57, 66, 83, 174
Beaux Arts, Ecole des, 11, 14, 20, 21, 22, 52, 57, 62
Belvedere Torso, The Vatican, 120
Benenson, Mary Watkins Camp, 38
Berg, Dr. Alberta and Berg, Dr. Henry W., 128
Berg Collection Room, 32, 128, 202

Berg Exhibition Room, 128
Bibliothèque Nationale, Paris, 150
Bigelow, John, 5, 44, 167
Billings, Dr. John Shaw, 6, 7, 8, 15, 33, 45, 151, 153, 163, 168, 184, 213
Blind Milton Dictating Paradise Lost *to His Daughters*, 133
Bonnard, Henry Company, 122, 213
Bosworth, Welles, 23
Bourbon Palace, Caserta, 90
Bowker, R. R., 41
Brenner, Victor David, 29, 196
Bronx War Memorial, Pelham Bay Park, 52
Brown, Henry Kirke, 183
Brown, Dr. Margaret, 78
Bryant Monument, 209, 210
Bryant Park, 15, 29, 32, 206–11
Bryant, William Cullen, 15, 29, 204, 207, 209
Butler Library, Columbia University, 150

Cadwalader, John L., 6, 7
Carlson, Chester, 106
Carnegie, Andrew, 6
Carrère & Hastings, xi, 8, 9, 10, 11, 14, 16, 19, 20, 24, 29, 37, 38, 41, 49, 52, 66, 69, 78, 98, 112, 116, 117, 119, 122, 141, 151, 158, 171, 176, 184, 193, 199, 205, 206, 210
Carrère, John Merven, 18, 19, 20, 22, 28, 29, 33, 45, 109, 213
Catalog Room, 33, 130, 137–42, 153, 155, 161
Cavaglieri, Giorgio, N.33
Cerocchi, Giuseppe, 183
Children's Division, 32
Clark, William A., Jr., Library, 83
Clarke, Gilmore, D. 210
Classical America, 17
Clerici, Leone, 78

Clodion (Claude Michel), 183
Codman, Ogden, Jr., 128, 141, 173, 175, 177
Cogswell, Joseph Green, 4, 6, 184
Colosseum, The, Rome, 142
Conservators' Hall, 196
Copley, John Singleton, 133
Corraia Lima, José Otavio, 210
Correggio (Antonio Allegri), 183
Coutan, Jules-Alexis, 179
Cox, Kenyon, 29
Croton Aqueduct System, 5
Cunard Building, 30, 112

Danby, Vermont, 16
Davidson, Jo, 109
Davis Brody Associates, N.33
Davis, Lewis, N.33
De Andrade Silva, José Bonifacio, 210
Declaration of Independence, 129
Decoration, The, of Houses, 128, 173, 175, 177
Delano, William Adams, 23
Delivery Desk, 146, 148, 149, 151
Derby Desk Company, Boston, 98
D'Espouy, Hector, 53
Detroit Public Library, 150
Dickens, Charles, 128
Dodge, William E., 210
Donnelly, John, 28
Donnelly & Ricci, 28
Dorset, Vermont, 16
Draper, Mrs. Henry, 133, 134
Durand, Asher B., 133

Economics and Public Affairs Divisions, 116
Eggers & Higgins, 32, 128
Ehrenkrantz Group, N.33
Eliot, Thomas Stearns, 128
Embury, Aymar, II, 32, 38, 128
Emmet, Ellen, 168

Farley, Archbishop John, 44
Farnese Palace, Salle D'Hercule, Rome, 158
Federal Hall Memorial, 16
Finn, James Wall, 141, 154
Fischer, Karl, 210
Flagg, Ernest, 5
Flagler, Henry Morrison, 22
Florida East Coast Railroad, 22
Founding Conservators, 196, Appendix V
Fragments From Greek and Roman Architecture, 53
Frees, Harry J., 210
French Academy in Rome, 14, 21
Frick Collection, 4, 16, 30, 49, 66

Gabriel, Ange-Jacques, 23, 52, 53, 112, 206, 207
Gaillon, Chateau de, 103
Ginain, Léon, 20
Goethe, Johann Wolfgang von, 210
Gorham Ornamental Bronze Company, 193
Gothicizers, The, 158
Gottesman, D.S. and R.H. Foundation, 78
Gottesman Exhibition Hall, 73–89, 148, 165, 183, 200, 201
Goujon, Jean, 199
Graff, Mrs. Robert D., 78
Grand Central Terminal, 35, 179
Grand Prix de Rome, 14, 21
Grand Trianon, Versailles, 41
Grandelli, Mr., 29, 41, 43
Grant Park, Chicago, 210
Green, Andrew Haswell, 5
Grieve, Maurice, 83, 213

Haas, Richard, 100
Hadley, Morris, 168
Halleck, Fitz-Greene, 4
Hamilton, Alexander, 183
Hamilton, Alexander II, 168
Hardouin-Mansart, Jules, 41
Harper's Magazine, 76

Harvard, Medical School, 16
Hastings, Thomas, 10, 18, 19,
  20, 22, 23, 28, 29, 30, 31, 33,
  41, 43, 45, 69, 83, 94, 188,
  213
Hastings, Reverend Thomas, 20
Haverstick, Mrs. Iola, 78
Hayes, Rutherford B., 4
Hofbibliothek, Hofburg,
  Vienna, 150
Hogarth, William, 40
Howard & Cauldwell, 8
Hughes, Robert Ball, 183
Hunt, Richard Morris, 4, 15, 19,
  20
Huntington, Daniel, 168, 187
Huntington, Dr. W. R., 44

Institute of Fine Arts, New
  York University, 66
Irving, Washington, 4, 183

James, Henry, 35
Jefferson, Thomas, 129, 183
Jennings, Oliver B., 183
Jewish Division, 196
Johansen, John, 168
John, Augustus, 133
Johnson, Eastman, 166

Karpen, S. & Brothers, 183
Kenan, William Rand, Jr., 166
Kennedy, John Stewart, 188
Kindred Spirits, 133
Kinnari, Theodore S., N.33
Kroll, Leon, 210

Lafayette, Marquis de, 133
Land, Edwin, 106
Laning, Edward, 126, 127
Ledyard, Lewis Cass, 6, 168
Lenox, James, 3, 4, 48, 129, 131,
  163
Lenox Library, 4, 188
Le Quesne, E., 184
Lescot, Pierre, 199
Letarouilly on Renaissance Rome,
  57, 83, 174
Leyendecker Brothers, 183
Library of Congress, The,
  Washington, D.C., 8, 180
Library Staff, World War I and
  World War II Veterans, 279
Lincoln Center, Performing
  Arts Research Center, 32
Lincoln Memorial, Washington,
  D.C., 59
Longworth and Cannon Office
  Buildings, Washington, D.C.,
  29
Lostis, John, 24, 213
Lostis & Neumann, 24
Louvre, The, Paris, 78, 89
Louvre, The, Henri II Room,
  Paris, 158
Louvre, The, Henry II Wing,
  Paris, 199
Low Library, Columbia Univer-
  sity, 112
Low, Seth, Mayor, 44, 197
Lowell, Josephine Shaw, Foun-
  tain, 210

McGraw, Harold W., Jr., 78
McKim, Charles Follen, 83
McKim, Mead & White, 8, 19,
  22, 28, 41
MacMonnies, Frederick, 22, 56,
  57, 188
Madrazo, Raimondo de, 167
Main Reading Room, xi, 14, 15,
  118, 145–59, 161, 207
*Man as Hero: The Human Figure
  in Western Art,* 17
Manhattan Bridge, New York,
  30
Mansart, François, 78
Map Division, 11, 104
Marble & Shattuck Company,
  Cleveland, 98, 99
Marchant, Edward Dalton, 112
Martiny, Philip, 27, 49
Massachusetts Institute of Tech-
  nology, 23
Menconi, Francesco, 29, 40, 41,
  43
Menconi, Raffaele, 29, 40, 41,
  43
Meridian Hill Park, Washing-
  ton, 210
Metropolitan Museum of Art,
  49, 103, 112, 188
Miami University, 6
Michelangelo, 55
Mid-Manhattan Branch, New
  York Public Library, 32
Milton, John, 145
Mitchel, John Purroy, 41
Morgan Library, 16
Morse, Samuel F. B., 131
Munkacsy, Mihaly, 133
Music, Dance and Theatre Col-
  lections and Divisions, 32

National Academy of Design,
  66
Neilson, Raymond, P. R., 168
Neumann & Even, 24, 184, 210
Newspaper Division, 104
New York Chamber of Com-
  merce, 16
New York Horticultural Soci-
  ety, 38
New York Stock exchange, 16
New-York Woodcarvers and
  Modelers Association, 24
North Stairway, The, 109

O'Neill, Rose, 156
Oriental Division, 112
O'Shea, Cornelius M., 205

Paine, Mrs. August G., 78
Paine, Mr. and Mrs. Peter, 78
Palace of the Conservators,
  Rome, 195, 196
Palazzo Mattei, Rome, 92
Palm Beach, Florida, 22
Palmer, Mrs. Carleton, 78
Parthenon, The, Athens, 59
Peale, James, 131
Peale, Rembrandt, 131
Peemans, G., 183
Performing Art Research Cen-
  ter, 32

Petit Trianon, Versailles, 206
Piccirilli Brothers, 38, 48
Pio Clementino Museum, The
  Vatican, 69
Piranesi, Giovanni Battista, 51,
  118, 193, 211
Pitman, Sir Isaac, 138
Place de la Concorde, Paris, 23,
  52, 206, 207, 211
Platt, Charles Adams, 210
Polaroid Camera, 106
Polk, Frank Lyon, 168
Pope, John Russell, 66
Ponce de Leon Hotel, St.
  Augustine, Florida, 22
Portico, The, 59–62
Potter, Edward Clark, 37, 38
Print Gallery, 129
Prints, Photographs and Spencer
  Collection, 128, 129
Proctor, Alexander Phimister,
  24, 53
Propylaea, on the Acropolis,
  Athens, 59
Pulitzer Fountain, 30
Purdom, Theo, N.33

Quinn, John, 133

Radtke, Martin, 69
Raeburn, Sir Joshua, 133
Rare Book Room, 129
Rauch, Daniel Christian, 127
Reader's Digest, The, 92
Reynolds, Sir Joshua, 133
Rice, Pierce, 17, 156, 183
Richmond, Virginia, Jefferson
  Hotel, 29
Rives, George Lockhart, 6
Robert, Hubert, 118
Rockefeller Brothers Fund, 78
Rockefeller, David, 163
Rockefeller, John D., Jr., 53
Room 80, 197, 198, 202
Rosario, Lorenzo, 29, 41, R.3
Rosenblatt, Arthur, N.33
Rubens, Peter Paul, 24
Ruskin, John, 158
Russell-Erwin Company, 79

Saint-Gaudens, Augustus, 37
St. John Lateran, Basilica,
  Rome, 158
Saint Mark's Square, Venice, 41
St. Peter's Basilica, Rome, 55
St. Peter's Square, Rome, 142
Salomon, Edna B., Room, 33,
  125, 129, 134
Science and Technology
  Research Center, 104, 106
Scudder, Janet, 29
Simpson, Lusby, 210
Slavonic Division, 112
Small, Herbert, 8
Smith, Edward R., 29
Soldiers and Sailors Monument,
  Brooklyn, 57
Standard Oil Trust, 22
South-North Gallery, 89–91
Staten Island, Borough Hall and
  Richmond County Court-
  house, 30

Statue of Liberty, The, 19
Sterling Library, Yale Univer-
  sity, 150
Stokes Gallery, 128, 202
Stokes, Isaac Newton Phelps,
  126, 128
Strong, William L., 197
Stuart, Gilbert, 131

Teniers, David III, 183
Thackery, William Makepeace,
  128
Third Floor Landing Hall, 125–
  27, 202
Tiepolo, Giovanni Battista, 24
Tiffany Studios, 29
Tilden, Samuel Jones, 3, 4, 48,
  187
Tilden Trust, 6
Tonetti-Dozzi, François M. L.,
  27, 49, 177
Trentanove, Raimondo, 129
Trustees' Room, 27, 171–85

United States History, Local
  History, and Genealogy Division, 161–63
University of California, Berkeley, 150
University of Illinois, Urbana,
  150
Uris Brothers Foundation, Inc.,
  78

Vanderbilt, William Kissam, 15,
  19
Van Wyck, Robert Anderson,
  197
Versailles, Palace of, 27, 52
Veterans, *see* Library Staff
Vignola (Giacomo Barozzi), 49,
  95
Villa Farnesina, Rome, 195, 196
Viollet-le-Duc, Eugène-
  Emmanuel, 158

Wallace, DeWitt, 92
Wallace, DeWitt, Periodical
  Room, 11, 28, 33, 89–104,
  146, 174, 184
Wallace, Lila Acheson, 92
Ward, J. Q. A., 210
Ware, William R., 8, 19, 173
Warren & Wetmore, 41, 141
Washington, George, 131
Wells, Joseph Morrill, 19
Wharton, Edith, 128, 173, 175,
  177
Whittier, John Greenleaf, 55
Widener Library, Harvard Uni-
  versity, 150
Woolf, Virginia, 128
Wordsworth, William, 196

Xerox, 106

Yale University, Memorial Hall,
  29
Young, Owen D., 128

Zawislan, Michael, 98, 213